Wings of Blue

Books by Michael Bleriot
Memories of an Emerald World
The Jungle Express
Wings of Blue
Flying Naked

Wings of Blue

MICHAEL BLERIOT

MacGregor Books, Inc

Washington DC MMXIII

Copyright © 2013 Michael Bleriot
All rights reserved.

No part of this book may be reproduced in any manner
whatsoever without written permission except in the case of
brief quotations embodied in critical articles or reviews.

The following is a work of fiction. Any resemblance
to persons living or dead is coincidental.

ISBN: 0983375143
ISBN-13: 978-0983375142
Library of Congress Control Number: 2012922113

Printed in the United States of America

To Ralph Ponticelli

Contents

	Preface	i
1	Wings of Blue	1
2	Ecuador	133
3	Idiots	189
4	Weather	211

PREFACE

THE C-27A SPARTAN WAS A twin-engine turboprop cargo plane used by the U.S. military in Central and South America during the 1990s. Modified from the Italian G-222, it was large enough to carry several tons of cargo and people but small enough to get into most of the airstrips scattered around the jungles of the region. That mission was called tactical airlift. For ten years the C-27 filled an essential airlift niche by supplying locations too remote for helicopters to reach and too small for bigger aircraft to land.

The C-27 wasn't sleek: a bulbous nose and squat fuselage made it look chubby – some compared it to a baby seal. But it was rugged enough to pound down onto rutted clearings carved into the forest and durable enough to bounce through thunderstorms over the Andes mountains. Crews routinely mistreated the airframe and engines by carrying too much, landing too hard, or driving it like an off-road vehicle through grass, gravel, sand, or mud. Many of the crews flying the "Mighty Chuck," as it was affectionately called, amplified their harsh treatment by being inexperienced. Others came to the plane with lots of hours in the air – and then misapplied lessons learned in other aircraft. Yet the C-27 never complained and always persevered. In a decade of operations it rarely broke, never crashed, and won accolades from those who had the privilege to fly aboard – in both the cockpit and the cabin.

The C-27 had one home, Howard Air Base in Panama. Crews also staged temporary operations from satellite fields in Honduras and Peru. From these locations they reached sites as far north as Guatemala and as far south as Bolivia, from the Pacific coast to the jungles of Brazil.

The C-27 fleet left Panama in 1999 when the United States gave the Canal Zone and its military bases to the country of Panama. The Air Force retired the planes shortly thereafter.

Wings of Blue

1. Wings of Blue

IN THE SUMMER OF 1990, a little-known fact of the United States Air Force was that it had no dedicated combat search-and-rescue flying units and hadn't since shortly after the Vietnam War. The Air Rescue Squadrons that became legends in Vietnam with their exploits and sacrifices in Hueys, Huskies, and Jolly Green Giants were a decade and a half later just a shadow of their former selves.

But while rescue pilots spent the fifteen years after Saigon's fall regressing to a peacetime role – following around fighter squadrons as they trained in case some F-16 driver needed to punch out – the ground component of the rescue services stayed ready for combat. These were the PJs, pararescue-jumpers, who were the Air Force's answer to Navy SEALs. Their close companions were combat controllers (CCT), who jumped into hostile territory to reconnoiter and then control forward airstrips.

Both PJs and CCT still trained hard and worked hard. They swam, jumped, ran, climbed mountains, and lived in tropical heat or mountain blizzards if that's what it meant to get a survivor to safety or find a place for aircraft to land. The PJs especially had regular opportunities to practice their skills since someone, somewhere, was always getting into a life-threatening situation and needing to be bailed out. Even in Panama, boating accidents, climbing mishaps, and snake-bites in the jungle kept them busy. Once we took a team 200 miles south of the Pearl Islands where they jumped into the water to help a yachtsman who'd been bitten in half by a great white shark. The boater didn't make it but that didn't stop the PJs from trying.

Their equipment wasn't the best. Budget cuts and a decade of forgetfulness by leaders more enamored with new planes and big projects fostered a make-do culture in the rescue world. Yet the quality of the personnel remained high, as did their morale. Both PJs and CCT kept their history alive on a daily basis. They knew the challenge to live up to it was never far away. As a result they were some of the most professional, skilled servicemen you would come across. In a service not known for tough, hard men, PJs and CCT earned the respect of the Army and Navy alike.

We didn't have a permanent squadron of PJs at Howard Air Base, the last remaining U.S. air base in Panama and except for a small airfield in Honduras the only one in all of Latin America. Instead there was a detachment of four or five guys who were supplemented by rotating groups of half a dozen who came through on 90-day tours and operated out of office space behind the parachute shop in Hangar 2. They boated and dove with the SEALs at Rodman Naval Station, which was over on the Canal. And they did recon patrols with our Army neighbors on Fort Kobbe. We only saw them when they wanted to make jumps from the C-27.

In early spring a group of PJs came through that Big Bud McIlhenny recognized. When they recognized him, his nightmares came back. His nightmares had nothing to do with the PJs and everything to do with jumping. More than anyone else in the squadron, I understood why.

Bud was borderline obsessive-compulsive. *Obsessive-compulsive* because he couldn't close his gear locker in the hangar unless the patches on the flight suits hanging there lined up perfectly; because his life was determined by even numbers – license plate, apartment address, even his social security ID; because all the pots and pans in his kitchen had their handles pointed to magnetic north; because any task started had to be finished. He drove at 20 mph, 40 mph, or 60 mph. He parked his car only on north-south streets. But he was *borderline* because he had lapses: he didn't get to pick which aircraft to fly on a given day, for example (some had odd serial numbers and those of us behind the scheduling desk weren't going to re-assign crews just to find a number four). Also, when it came to *wearing* his uniform no one could accuse him of being all right angles and tight corners. When Lowell dropped Pick-up Sticks in front of Bud to see him react, most of the time he shrugged it off.

Bud was Big Bud because we had another Bud in the squadron: Bud Blair. Blair, Little Bud, was the size of a jockey and suffered from an aggressive short guy complex. Even without alcohol he was a hyperactive pain in the ass but put one beer in him and he would puff out his chest and strut around the room challenging tall guys to a fight. He and Bud were as different as night and day and they hated each other. Or at least Little Bud hated Big Bud, particularly after their first encounter where Little Bud wanted to fight and Big Bud simply put a hand on his forehead, holding him at arm's length while Little Bud swung wild, helpless punches. Blair, confounded by Big Bud's silence, fell back on the standard man-insult, stating his belief that Big Bud was gay. And since few people had ever been to Big Bud's apartment or even knew where he lived, Little Bud insisted he was also homeless, living on the streets of Panama City. "He's a homo hobo!" Blair would announce and then fall over drunk. Fortunately for him his nemesis was a patient man.

He was also an expert parachutist. Big Bud was a Zoomie, meaning he had gone to the Air Force

Academy. He had earned his jump wings there and been on its demonstration team, the Wings of Blue. In fact he had been on track to break the Academy record for number of jumps until a couple of incidents gave him a brush with mortality that he preferred not to re-visit. On the first a malfunctioning canopy caused him to go to his reserve, which also malfunctioned but opened enough to let him land on the side of a hill where instead of becoming part of the landscape he only broke two bones in his right leg. On the second, preparing for his record-breaking day, he collided with a teammate. The crash knocked both of them unconscious but they were saved when their altitude-triggered automatic openers popped their chutes for them a mere ten seconds before impact. Again Bud broke bones but this time the real damage was psychological. Passing out while falling and then waking up on the ground messed with his head in a big way.

For days afterward he tossed and turned, tortured with the idea of quitting, of giving up on the record, of having a glass half-empty for the rest of his life but plagued by a fear so strong he could touch it. In his mind his next trip out the door would be his last, the ground screaming up at him getting bigger and bigger until there was nothing else to see while he scrabbled for his chute and came up empty-handed. When he dreamed at night he saw ground and air. When he woke in the morning he trembled.

After his injuries healed he announced he would still jump on graduation day. Then he drove to the field and backed down. Just seeing a parachute made him shake. He couldn't take it and he quit the team entirely, one free-fall short of the record, convinced that life in limbo was better than death in a messy pile.

Excruciating doesn't describe his decision. A normal person would live on with a nagging ache of guilt, a dull sense of a job not finished that would fade away as time went on and pop up only in such rearward-looking moments as mid-life crises and retirement. But for Bud it was as though Damocles' sword had already fallen and sliced him through lengthwise. One jump to break the Academy record – a brilliant capstone to a parachutist's career! Worse, that same jump would put him at a thousand. A thousand jumps in four years. Four years to the day if he jumped at graduation. Ten to the third power – a solid round number to soothe his orderly id. Everyone at the Academy encouraged him to reconsider. Some thought he was crazy to give up so close.

Maybe he was. Then again, Bud's presence on the team alone made some people say "hmmm." At first glance he wasn't the kind of guy you would think would be on a demonstration team for anything except maybe a vagabond troupe of tense Russian chess players. You didn't need Bud Blair to point out that the Wings of Blue, like other Air Force public relations units such as the Thunderbirds and the marching band, tended to look gay. Their immaculate, form-fitting jump suits and '70s-style haircuts, as well as the fact that most members were tall white males, made one wonder upon seeing them if the Church of Latter Day Saints hadn't formed its own armed service. Big Bud, by contrast, was lanky, stooped, and had cheeks scarred by acne. Though in addition to parachuting he also swam at inter-collegiate meets he didn't have the build or swagger of an athlete. He walked in a distracted fashion, an absent-minded genius who worried more about things like plastic not being bio-degradable and whether *pi* had a finite number of decimal places than about how to look good for a camera. No one pictured him as an Air Force poster child. Though male and white, he blended in with the Academy Ken-dolls like Karl Marx at a Wall Street brokerage.

But then Bud was a strange guy about whom you could have said "hmmm" for a lot of reasons. He rarely smiled. His constant worrying gave him gray hair at 25. It stuck up straight on his head and had the appearance of a mowed lawn. Some of his worries came from being obsessed, some came from relatives. His parents were unreformed flower children who divorced and remarried several times and who collected foster children the way other people gather refrigerator magnets, which meant that Bud grew up never quite sure who was his sibling and who had just been dropped off by the state.

Hmmm.

At the Academy Bud double-majored in aeronautical engineering and naval architecture, challenging fields that suited his demand for completion and closure but that worked him hard along the way. The pressure of his classes found outlets in unusual ways. There was the time he spent the night hanging inverted from a chapel rafter to determine for himself if Bernoulli's conclusions on hydrodynamics worked the same for blood vessels as they did for water. Or the time a senior ordered him to sing the Air Force song and Bud did – backwards and in key. The pinnacle was when he built a scale replica of a Viking longboat in his dormitory room. The boat was so large it couldn't fit through the door or window. People couldn't enter, either – which was fine for most since Bud demanded a conversation in Old Norse before he would grant permission anyway. When campus security finally declared the boat a fire hazard and came to remove it, Bud held off the guards for hours by jamming the door shut with home-made oars and wielding a bust of Erik the Red as a weapon. A disciplinary board and school psychologist eventually found him eccentric but harmless and sent him on to pilot training – which for years set junior cadets to thinking of odd behavior they could use to guarantee a pilot's slot for themselves.

Hmmm.

From pilot training Bud graduated to a KC-135 tanker. Flying racetracks in the sky grew boring, though, and he spent only a year in the refueling business before heading down to Panama.

In our squadron his first additional duty was at the scheduling desk with me. It was an arrangement I found difficult. We were both new and learning the job together which meant that sometimes we fell behind and had to do hectic crisis management to keep a mole-hill of paperwork from becoming a mountain of missed deadlines. But Bud wasn't good at crisis management. Crisis management meant moving quickly and that was something he just didn't do. To Bud every task was a mystery of other, hidden tasks each of which required careful consideration. Opening a spread-sheet on the computer, for example, became an extended study of the programming that put the spread-sheet there in the first place. This tendency toward deconstructionist analysis was amusing and would have been useful had we been, say, planning a protracted land campaign in China. But we weren't. All I wanted to do was match flyers with airplanes for next week.

So Bud moved up to the mobility shop, a one-man-deep office where he could indulge his predilection for details and even numbers. A squadron's mobility shop prepares a unit to pick up and move in its entirety when a contingency requires. The fact that the 155th Tactical Airlift Squadron didn't need a mobility shop, that by being in Panama we were already a forward-deployed unit and could accomplish our mission by sending planes in ones and twos in all directions, never registered with anyone, certainly not with Bud. The Air Force required every squadron to have a mobility office so we did. Bud ran it like a German train schedule, too, keeping meticulous track of every assigned person, plane, and piece of equipment and constantly updating his grandiose schemes to move us to places like Burundi, Korea, and Lapland should the situation require – which the situation never did. In my three years in the squadron, Burundi and Lapland remained calm and Korea never beckoned. But because he had a world where detail reigned supreme and every plan had a beginning and an end, Bud finally had reason to be happy.

We assumed, therefore, that he *was* happy – or rather nobody gave it enough thought to assume he wasn't. It was hard to tell because it was hard to get close to the guy. He was always busy and always thinking, walking with head down staring at the floor as though he was just about to remember where he had dropped his keys.

In the squadron he came and went and moved around and did his job. He wasn't the kind who would hang around the scheduling desk to chat. He would *stop* at the scheduling desk if people were there but always stood quietly to the side, listening and nodding in agreement but rarely chipping in his two cents. General conversation drew him out not at all. A query of "Anybody do anything interesting over the weekend?" sailed past him as though afraid to enter his ears. You had to speak to him directly – "Bud, what did *you* do last night?" and even then he would parse words like a chastened Calvin Coolidge. Talking to him was the verbal equivalent of dragging a body up a hill.

Bud knew the PJs from Key West, Florida. Actually, he met them at Homestead Air Force Base just north of Key West. Homestead was where all the services sent their troops for water survival training. In one mixed course all kinds of people could come together. That Bud met the PJs at all was itself a coup.

The PJs are junior members of the Special Forces and don't take in just anybody as a friend. They're "junior members" because the term SF applies in full only to Army Green Berets and Navy SEALs. (Even Army Rangers aren't considered SF by anybody but other Rangers.) As such they have to be careful who they're seen with to avoid being dragged back down to the conventional level by association. Hanging out with the "blue-suiter" Air Force could make real tough guys think PJs were weak. It's all image and all silly but in the military it matters. Everybody wants to be unique and the ranks of SF troops are no different.

There's an old joke about a snake that illustrates the differences in perspective of the various units around the military that claim to be "special":

A venomous snake appears in the middle of a forest path...

The Rangers charge forward in battalion-strength, blindly machine-gunning everything they see until the snake is dead, the snake's family is dead, every animal within two miles is dead, and the entire forest is a charred, smoldering hole.

> *Marine recon teams, dressed as a copse of saplings, watch the snake for days before suggesting an amphibious assault further up the coast to attack it. If no coast is nearby, the Marines move the snake closer to a coast.*
>
> *The Green Berets move in with the snake, befriend it, sympathize with its cause, and then teach it to kill other snakes.*
>
> *Navy SEALs parachute in under the cover of night, kill the snake in a stealthy manner preferably using an expensive dive knife, then call in a naval bombardment to make sure it's dead.*
>
> *Combat controllers note the flat piece of ground near the snake that could be used as an assault landing strip where a battalion of Rangers could be infiltrated. If no flat piece of ground is available, CCT moves the snake closer to one.*
>
> *And the PJs? Well, they shoot the snake and then spend hours working to save its life.*

Their notch in the SF tier being thus razor-thin, PJs relate more readily to other ground forces than to members of their own service. They don't expect to be impressed by a pilot. After all, an important element of their identity is that they and combat controllers are the only Air Force personnel who prefer to exit airplanes before they land. And then there's their skill in water. PJs swim. And swim. And swim and swim and swim. Even Navy SEALs hold PJs in high regard for their ability to save people on the water, in the water, under the water, and anywhere near water. Those two skills set them apart from everyone else in the service tasked with dominating the air.

So when Bud showed up at Homestead boasting not only jump wings but an awe-inspiring ability to knife through waves like a tuna late for school, the PJs decided he was alright. So much so that they invited him out for a night on the town in Key West.

Key West is a party town. Jimmy Buffett didn't settle there because of the work ethic. It's tropical, has great beaches and hot weather, and boasts more bars and nightclubs per square mile than anywhere else on the East Coast. For some reason, it also has a large gay population.

Big Bud was having a beer with Clegg (a Green Beret) and two PJs at a bar called The Pink Parrot when up walked one of the many buff, tight-t-shirt-wearing local men gathered in the joint. The quartet of Rangers seated nearby ignored him, as did Bud and his friends. But buff boy started up a conversation with Clegg and proceeded to hit on him. Clegg, unfazed, politely turned him away and went back to drinking his beer. The local then hit on the PJs who, being

Air Force, at first were flattered but eventually expressed their disinterest.

When the local turned to the Rangers one of them knocked him cold. "Aw, shit," said Clegg, and quickly finished his beer.

Suddenly, the huge number of homosexuals that nobody had noticed in the bar until that moment all looked up as their friend hit the floor. They put down their drinks and advanced toward the Rangers. There were some large men in the pack and all were ready to avenge their fallen pal. When the Rangers finally noticed the advancing crowd, even they were taken aback.

Clegg decided the best defense was a good offense. He grabbed the Rangers' table and flipped it in front of the menacing crowd.

"You want some of this, poof boys?!! Bring it on!"

And the crowd did. The locals attacked en masse. Clegg leveled the first two like a berserk logger felling trees, his victims falling over the already prone body of the love-struck bodybuilder who had started it all. Then he stepped back to let the Rangers do their cannon-fodder work. The Rangers, figuring out that a fight was in progress and that they'd better hurry if they didn't want to miss it, waded in in full fury, each taking on as many of the enemy as they could in order to have bragging rights later.

Big Bud and the PJs helped out where they could, slugging away with the Rangers until they realized a more effective tactic was to hurl chairs at the back of the surging mass of gays to discourage the expanding crowd of participants. Clegg, being true SF, went for the crowd's base of power. He picked up one table after another and flung it over the bar at the taps and liquor bottles behind. Glass flew and the lights overhead flickered. The bartenders ran for cover. The owner of the bar screamed for help until one of his own customers laid him out with a wild punch.

"The door! The door!" the PJs yelled and started working what ground forces call a "retrograde action" toward the exit. Big Bud went along with the retreat, gouging and head-butting his way across the room. Clegg, too, followed but only after the last strategic target had disintegrated beneath his artillery assaults and he was left with the more mundane task of eliminating attackers one by one. The Rangers, cursing, laughing, and swinging the whole time, were reluctant to leave their element. It wasn't until the wail of sirens was heard above the riot that they finally broke lock and followed everyone else out into the street.

"This way!" shouted Clegg, pointing to the right, whereupon the Rangers immediately took off running to the left. Since that was the direction of the sirens, Clegg was left shaking his head in exasperation.

Bud and the PJs, instinctively thinking that any direction the Army chose had to be wrong, ran off straight ahead and instantly regretted it as they were thus the first thing the crowd of gays caught sight of upon emerging from the bar. Clegg was left on his own and walked home in peace.

It then came down to a foot race: Big Bud and the two PJs versus what seemed like half of Key West's population.

"Right!"

"No, left!"

"That's worse!"

"I lost my beer!"

"Get off the street!"

"There! Through there!"

Eventually, even with several drinks in them Bud and the PJs gained distance from the mob. Then they ran out of island and had to turn back whereupon the hunt began again, this time with the PJs directing a perilous game of hide-and-seek around the fishing shacks, kiosks, and bars that lined the main drag. Whenever they thought they'd eluded the pack entirely, yet another Parrot customer would spot them and sound the alert.

Then one of the PJs sobered up and had his first clear thought.

"Where's the water?"

That was like asking a pig to find truffles. Big Bud took the lead and two streets later they were at the wharf. The gays spread out so they were seen again but now Bud had a plan: if they swam across the bay the mob would be forced to go around the long way. They could finally escape. So the three of them dove into the dark water and started swimming.

That was how the PJs knew Bud.

How I knew Bud was a different matter.

In my first months in Panama there was a pilot named Howell in the squadron, a captain and former C-130 pilot from an air base in Japan. Howell came south in the "initial cadre" of instructors, the randomly-seasoned stew of Herc pilots who were chosen by God-knew-who to welcome the C-27 to the ranks of the military. He was neither a bad guy nor a bad pilot but he was a bit of a goof who displayed precarious judgment at the wrong times. Even to a new guy like me it was obvious that our commander, Lt Col Rasmussen, once he settled in and decided to cull the ranks, had Howell slated for the chopping block.

We all thought it would happen in mid-August when Howell thought it would be funny to wear a set of Doctor Dudley's false teeth (which made him look like a British pensioner) during the SOUTHCOM commander's visit to the squadron. But Rasmussen held back. He must have known that a better, unimpeachable reason to send Howell packing was only a matter of time.

On the last day of August Walt corralled me to hop on a day flight for airdrop training.

"Don't worry," he said. "It's a HALO drop. All you have to do is hold the plane straight and level at 10,000 feet. You can do that, can't you?"

"HALO?"

"High Altitude, Low Opening. We open the door, the jumpers run out the back and freefall to 2,000 feet. Nothing to it."

"If you say so."

At the last minute Howell showed up and asked to fly. Walt said no but Howell persisted. Finally Walt agreed to let him get some right-seat time after the SEAL drop.

There really was nothing to the HALO. We took off with eight SEALs in the back and flew out over the Pacific in a giant arc around Taboga Island. In a blue and empty sky with a cobalt sea below we climbed to ten thousand feet and leveled off. Then we headed inland toward the drop zone just west of Howard Air Base. In the back the SEALs sprawled around the floor catching a nap.

"Give the team five minutes," Walt called to Bird, our loadmaster.

"Copy," came the reply. There was shouting in the back, then the report, "the team has five minutes."

At Bird's yell the SEALs got to their feet and stretched. They went from one to another checking parachute harnesses, rip cords, and helmets. Then they lay back down for a few more minutes of sleep.

Bird cleared any loose items from the cabin and prepared to lower the cargo ramp. To keep himself from falling out when he opened the door, he clicked himself into a harness attached to a tie-down ring on the floor. The harness had a strap that was only long enough to let Bird reach the edge of the ramp – i.e., he couldn't accidentally tumble out. Howell, who was also in the cabin, didn't have a harness so instead he put on one of the crew parachutes that normally hung on the wall for us to use in an emergency. Safety regulations and common sense said anyone in the cabin had to wear one or the other whenever a door was open.

"Three minutes," Walt called.

"Copy." Through my earphones I heard Bird yelling to the team leader, who was no longer on headset. Again he reported back, "The team has three minutes."

Walt held us in a crab due to westerly winds as we approached the coast. Our course would take us a mile west of Howard's runway and directly over the large meadow that was the drop zone. At two minutes he passed the controls to me and put his hand up by the ramp control switch.

"Clear to open the door?" he asked into the mike.

"Clear!" Bird replied.

"Door's coming open."

As the cargo door swung up and the ramp came down, the only thing we noticed up front was a little more noise and light in the cabin. I had to push forward ever so slightly on the controls to hold the nose down as ten people in back moved aft toward the open door.

"One minute," said Walt.

"Team has one!"

The coast disappeared beneath the windscreen, then reappeared in the small window by my feet. I clenched the controls, willing myself not to do anything that would cause problems for the jumpers.

"Ten seconds," said Walt, and put his hand by the Drop Signal switch. When he flipped it up, a green light would illuminate over our heads. Another green light would come on in the back of the cabin by the ramp. He had figured our release point carefully and would leave the light on as long as a dropped object could reasonably hit the zone. Once we were out of parameters he would flip the switch back down, changing the green light to red.

"Green light!"

There was a yell in unison from the cabin as the eight SEALs, leaning forward against each other, charged off the ramp with whoops and hollers. In a second they were gone, pounding feet and rushing bodies vanishing into the light as though they'd never been. Bird, his harness taut as he leaned out to look, and Howell, standing at the edge of the ramp unrestrained but with his parachute, watched the black silhouettes get smaller and smaller as they plunged toward the lush backdrop of the ground.

And then Howell jumped.

"Red light!"

So Rasmussen fired him.

The jump went fine. Howell landed only a little off target, by the tree line east of the dirt track that led into the middle of the DZ where all the SEALs had landed. His round standard-issue parachute looked lonely and incongruous floating down among the sporty, rectangular canopies of the SEALs but he plopped into the long grass and bounced up like just another member of the team.

Later he couldn't explain exactly why he had decided to leap into the slipstream. Talking to him it wasn't clear that he had decided at all. The closest I got to understanding was his description of how beautiful the ground looked from ten thousand feet: the deep blues of the water meeting the emerald green of the jungle, all beneath a golden sun and breathtakingly clear, clean air. The heat of the jungle reached up even to ten thousand feet and imparted warmth and sweetness that beckoned like a Siren to lonely sailors of the high thin air. That, combined with vertigo and the adrenalin rush of watching eight warriors practice their craft and knowing you're only inches away from joining them, teetering on an open ramp and needing only to let go and take one step, just one step, an easy step...

But it was stupid. Tempting, yes. Ballsy, yes. Smart, not at all. Even in a cowboy unit in Central America you don't just throw yourself out of an airplane without briefing with the other jumpers, coordinating with the crew, and – of course – getting permission from your commander. Doing so violates both the judgment and discipline commandments that any squadron leader brings down the mountain first. So Rasmussen sent Howell back to the States.

However, Howell's jump inspired me. From the moment Bird yelped and Walt and I stared at each other in astonishment, I admired the move. Would I have done it myself? No – at least I hope not. But I understood it. It was a spur of the moment, seize-the-day, wild and crazy stunt and it reminded me that I needed more of that adventure in my life.

So I quietly asked around to see where I could take skydiving lessons. Nobody in the squadron knew but the civilian mechanics across the way in Hangar 2 did. They were such an eclectic mix of seasoned, vagabond thrill-seekers themselves that I could have suggested bow-hunting yetis and either they would have already done it themselves, known somebody who'd done it, or at least had a lead on where I could take classes. For parachuting, they all pointed me to Vince.

Vince was the grand old man of our contract mechanics. He was neither grand nor old but he had been in Panama longer than anybody else and seemed to know everything there was to know about the country. Bald and fiercesomely mustached, he had a vague reputation for smuggling guns as a side job. He also pimped from time to time and had enjoyed a short-lived but staggeringly successful career servicing Canal tankers with Chorillo hookers before local authorities shut him down so they could compete for the same market.

Vince also jumped. That was all I knew or cared about. He belonged to a Panamanian skydiving club and normally did two or three jumps every Sunday to an abandoned runway halfway up the isthmus at Calzada Larga. The club was Panamanian, he told me, but a few ex-pats belonged and a few Army guys from Fort Clayton even showed up. At the moment he couldn't teach me himself because of a sore back he had earned while swapping out a motor on a friend's plane. But he enthusiastically hooked me up with a replacement instructor.

The replacement was a local named Alvaro. Small with dark skin, a big nose, and hair like a scrub brush, Alvaro limped but I couldn't tell on which leg. Sometimes he seemed to limp on both. He smiled a lot in a manner best described as concerned friendliness. Worry was his primary facial feature. His movements were jerky and repetitive. When he spoke he repeated himself, too. Everything about him radiated a concern that he wasn't covering all his bases. At first this annoyed me but later it was comforting. After all, I wanted the person who was teaching me to fall to earth to be anxious as hell.

Alvaro admitted that he rarely jumped anymore himself. He gestured toward his legs and

I didn't ask for details. He seemed to know a lot about parachuting nonetheless. Parachuting for beginners, in particular. He finished each lesson with a single declarative sentence that he implied would see me through safely should I forget everything else he'd taught that day. "Jettison, then Reserve," for example, or "If you tumble, relax before trying to pull." Deviations from his lessons weren't allowed. If I asked him something that he hadn't planned to cover, he ignored the question. When he skipped over exiting the aircraft by saying, "When you are clear of the aircraft..." and I asked for more specifics, he waved my words away like they were pesky flies.

Alvaro trained me in a week. Early in the morning for seven days we met at the *Parque Recreativo* off Calle 68 Este. It was quiet there, our only company parrots in the trees and the occasional lone coatimundi foraging through the overgrown grass. It was onto that grass that Alvaro had me jump from picnic tables to practice PLFs (Parachute Landing Falls). Later I graduated to jumping from trash cans, then to trash cans balanced on picnic tables. Within ten minutes every day my clothes were invariably soaked from both the effort and from the dew that clung to the lawn. He also brought out a parachute and unfolded it on the grass to identify the panels, the center seam, the four lines that when jettisoned gave me greater forward speed and more control, the risers, the ripcord, and the toggle for the emergency chute. He taught me to fold the parachute myself – again and again and again. It was all interesting at first but eventually grew arduous. After a week of doing nothing but look at silk and cord and wear out my legs jumping off trash cans, never once having seen a plane, I was convinced he and Vince were playing an elaborate joke just to make me look stupid. One day Alvaro finally took me by the Paitilla airport to meet some club members but even that was frustrating: only a few instructors showed up, and when they learned I didn't have even a single jump to my credit conversation stalled.

So the club was full of strangers, Alvaro was stringing me along, Vince I didn't know well enough to ask for more advice, and no one in the squadron seemed interested in my new hobby. I felt adrift.

One day I lamented my situation to Major Harmon, my workout-obsessed supervisor, who nodded absently as he did curls with a ninety-pound barbell that he kept behind the scheduling desk.

"So what do you think, sir?" I concluded, having expressed my concern that Alvaro was a fraud.

"I think I need a bigger weight," Harmon said proudly. "I just did two sets *reealll* slow and can hardly feel it. I'm not getting as vascular as I should."

"I meant about the skydiving. Should I keep up with it or is this guy just wasting my time?"

"What guy?"

"Alvaro. The guy I just...oh, never mind."

"Oh, him. Yeah, he's wasting your time. Probably just stretching out the lessons to collect his money and hoping you'll drop out before he has to go through the trouble of actually putting you on a plane. I would dump him."

"Really?"

"Look, Mike," Harmon said, rolling his weight away under the desk. "If you want adventure you should lift. Hit the gym. Pump some iron. I get a rush every time I look in the mirror. Check this out."

He struck a pose with both arms curled above his head. It revealed biceps like softballs that someone had injected into his arms. They rode back and forth between his elbow and shoulder like confused puppies under a blanket as he twisted his wrists one way and another. Harmon completely forgot about me as he stared at his own muscles, mesmerized.

"You jumping?" said a soft voice. It was Big Bud. He had walked up and been so quiet we hadn't noticed him.

"No, that's the trouble. So far I've done everything but jump."

"Where?"

I repeated my story.

"When are you supposed to go to the field?" he asked when I finished.

"Sunday. Eight o'clock in the morning. Alvaro said *maybe* I would get to go."

"Mind if I come along?"

I could have hugged him.

Sunday morning dawned with the standard brilliant blue sky I had almost but not quite grown accustomed to in Panama. I awoke at six and wolfed a quick breakfast.

When I pulled up to Big Bud's apartment in El Dorado he was waiting at the curb dressed in pressed khaki shorts and a linen shirt, looking for all the world like a British aristocrat on safari.

"You know how to get there?" he asked, putting a cooler in the back seat.

"Alvaro drew me a map," I replied and held out a napkin with some scribbles that my instructor had given me. Bud studied it and repeated his question. I shrugged.

What I knew was how to get to the Trans-Isthmian highway. There were no signs for that but just as I got home each night by turning right at the bus station and left at the La Cascada restaurant there were landmarks that we all used to travel north. Today Bud and I drove to the Canal and turned right, then cruised along the long stretch that wound past Fort Clayton and up to the Miraflores Locks. That road split before Gamboa – a tiny collection of early-century houses – and when it did we veered right to avoid Contractors Hill. Then we headed away from the Canal and drove several miles along a two-lane road that squeezed between the National Park and the Summit Botanical Gardens. Eventually we found the Trans-Isthmian highway and headed north toward Colón.

Alvaro's map depicted the highway as a squiggly line with x's alongside to mark features he considered important. But he hadn't specified what those features were. The x's could be towns or police checkpoints or billboards – anything. Bud had trouble dealing with the lack of precision.

"How far is this x from this x?" he asked.

"I have no idea."

"Well, is this curve to scale?"

"To scale?"

"Yes, is it to scale? It looks big compared to the distance he shows us coming from town. Does that mean the road arcs around to the east or is it just some turn he wanted us to expect before getting to this bridge?"

"Um, Bud, I think you're reading too much into the drawing. For all I know the curve is there because his pencil slipped."

"Well, this map leaves a lot of questions."

"Wait until you meet the guy who drew it."

The one definite turnpoint marked on the map was a road T halfway between Chilibre and Buenavista. After much trouble we found that spot and finally turned off the Colon highway.

The new road dipped sharply away from the highway and crossed a creek at a gravel ford. Then it topped a hill and pressed on for a mile in the direction of the canal. After a while it lost its pavement and turned to dirt, then to washboard dirt, then to broken, rolling, axle-breaking dirt. I drove slowly and maneuvered around the biggest potholes. Trees lined the road and met overhead, keeping us in shadow. We passed shacks and houses, most with garden plots and occasionally a horse or cow staked on a tether. Chickens clucked along the road.

"I think that's it," Bud announced. He pointed to a turnoff that led up an embankment and topped out somewhere beyond our sight.

I had my doubts but urged the Jimmy to make the effort. Whining in first gear it climbed between stands of sawgrass at an angle steep enough that we couldn't see over the hood. Twelve feet up we popped out into the light.

The top of the embankment was the edge of a long green plateau – the airfield of Calzada Larga. We found ourselves at the approach end of the abandoned runway. Its asphalt surface stretched toward us from the far side of the field and petered out yards away. In the distance several cars and a lone aircraft were parked in the grass. A windsock flew in the breeze, sticking up above an assortment of bright colors that waved and flapped as members of the Parachute Club folded their chutes and prepared for the first jump of the day. Except for them and the runway itself the plateau was empty. It was a huge lawn bordered by jungle.

We drove down the strip toward the gathering. Alvaro hobbled over as I parked. He was happy to see me and worried at the same time.

"Mike, Miguel, good morning, good morning. You came after all. I thought maybe you might not come. Maybe you might change your mind. Did you change your mind?"

I introduced Big Bud, who surveyed the scene carefully and with some reluctance. His eyes lingered longest on the silk canopies stretched in the grass and he soon wandered off to see them up close.

There were forty people clustered around the windsock. Next to it they had erected a tent to block the sun. Of those forty, half engaged in setting up equipment for a jump. Some folded and inspected chutes, others donned overalls and helmets, others did neither but sat in the grass and chatted. The rest of the crowd had no intention of jumping: they were girlfriends and boyfriends and relatives and neighbors along solely to enjoy a day in the country. A beagle chased a dachshund around the tent. Except for the battered Cessna 206 we could have been mistaken for a church picnic. There was nothing around the airstrip but fields and farms. When the breeze blew just right we could hear a cow lowing miles away.

Most of the people were locals. As Vince promised, though, the Army was represented: six white guys with farmer's tans and crew cuts crawled around the grass inspecting their equipment. There was also a middle-aged German named Gunter and a Nicaraguan doctor who looked entirely too prim and proper for the day's activity but still suited up for a jump.

Piza was there, too. Piza was a large, overweight twenty-something Panamanian who jumped in the club but who also, like Alvaro, made money on the side by teaching students. I had met him at Paitilla. Vince didn't trust him but Piza seemed alright to me. His right leg was still healing under a cast that went from his ankle to his hip. A month earlier after a day of jumping he had raced back to the city on his motorcycle with his parachute strapped to his back. Somewhere on the Via Brasil the pilot chute caught a breeze and deployed into the slipstream. One moment Piza was leaning over the handlebars watching for potholes and pedestrians and the next he was fifty feet in the air watching his new motorcycle careen down the street without him.

"I got one good swing," he acknowledged – before crashing into a Bimbo Bread truck going the opposite direction. His bike found a lamp post a block further on and was demolished.

Today he and a partner had the soldiers as their students. They walked the grunts through their maneuvers in the grass, explaining in good but limited English how they should arch, when they should pull, what they should do if they had trouble, etc. The soldiers paid attention.

I was nervous. The butterflies that had been in my stomach all morning now multiplied.

There were thirty people ready to jump. The Cessna 206 could carry only six so the club used a larger Twin Otter to carry the bulk of the load. While Alvaro prepared my equipment that second plane came in to land. It touched down gently on the old asphalt and taxied in close to the tent.

While the 206 loaded up, Alvaro excused himself. As senior organizer of the club, he hobbled across the grass to confer with the pilots.

Bud came back from his survey. The blank look was gone. Now his brow was furrowed and his face thoughtful. He looked like an accountant mulling over an audit.

"What do you think?" I asked, wanting to hear a positive assessment.

"Is that your chute?" He pointed at the one sitting on the ice chest by my feet.

"Yes."

"May I take a look?"

"Are you kidding? Take the damned thing apart, if you want. Tell me it'll work."

He knelt down and flipped the chute over, inspecting the bag. He opened the outer flaps and inspected as much of the risers, lines, cables, and silk as he could. After that he stared at the grass.

"May I have your keys?"

I handed him my car keys. He walked to the Jimmy, opened the trunk, and pulled out two drop clothes that I kept for my frequent trips to the auto hobby shop.

Bud found a sun-washed piece of grass away from the crowd where the dew had already evaporated. He spread out the drop cloths so that one overlapped the other and the two covered a good-sized piece of ground. Then he came back for my chute and lugged it over. He pulled out the lead chute, then the main chute, and spread them wide on the tarps. Unfolding and refolding with quick, precise movements, he inspected everything in the bags.

"Technically," he said quietly while he worked, "this is a breach of protocol. This is not my parachute, I'm not jumping with it, and I don't even know the people who folded it. Good jumpers trust each other."

I didn't know what to say to that so said nothing. Alvaro was still talking to the pilots and hadn't seen us take apart the chute. But I trusted Bud more than I trusted him. Breach any protocol you want, buddy, I thought.

When the canopy and all the risers were back in the bag Bud turned his attention to the shoulder and leg straps and rip cords. Then he studied the buckles like a metallurgist. His expression never changed. Calm, detached, studious.

Finally he stood up.

"It'll work," he said.

I felt a sandbag rise from my shoulders. If I died now at least it wouldn't be because of equipment malfunctions. I shook his hand with relief.

But Bud didn't look as happy as I felt. He stood with hands in his pockets watching in displeasure the blissful disarray of people, canopies, barbecue grills, and slobbery dogs. His personality was eccentric but where risk-taking was involved he verged on paranoia. The Panamanian Babel-approach to skydiving clearly bothered him.

"You see that fellow there," he said without pointing.

"Which one?"

"That one. The one lying in the grass? On his parachute?"

"Yes."

"Don't ever do that. Don't *ever* do that. That grass is still wet. All that moisture is right now seeping into his pack and into his chute. If he gets enough in there the silk will stick together and not deploy right. And if he doesn't jump for some reason and puts it away like that the silk will rot. You want to jump with a rotted chute?"

"Let me think. No?"

"That's why I put out the drop cloths. They're folding their chutes on the *ground*. It'll be another hour before this stuff is dry." He pushed the grass around with the toe of his shoe. Anywhere there was shade dew clung to the blades like honey to a comb.

"You see that guy?"

He nodded toward a fellow whose name I remembered was Lonny. Lonny was American: pale skin, long brown hair tied in a ponytail, moderately hippie. He was a Zonie gone local, the child of gringo parents who had grown up in the Canal Zone and then moved downtown. As Bud and I talked Lonny stretched his canopy on the grass and aligned the risers.

"Yeah. More moisture?"

"Yes. That and he's not using a cover. And he's doing it in the shade where the dew's going to stick longer. If he has to inspect his chute here he should do it in the sun and with a blanket or something under the canopy. The last thing you want is a twig or stone wrapped up in there where it can chafe and tear things."

Bud pointed out other safety lapses: club members wearing sandals, one sporting a leather World War 1-era flying helmet – stylish but pointless from a protective standpoint. Most jumpers had sunglasses instead of goggles.

"A little uncontrolled, huh?" I offered. Not knowing what was right or completely wrong, I could observe a questionable procedure and accept the explanation that "that's how things are done." Big Bud knew better.

"Just so much...attitude," he muttered. The brittle straw that was his hair trembled with disapproval. "Attitude without knowledge. Without discipline. It's dangerous. How many people get hurt here?"

The question startled me. I hadn't thought of it in such stark terms.

"I don't know."

"A lot, I'm guessing."

We stood in silence for a while.

Without thinking, I blurted out, "You ever going to jump again?"

Immediately I regretted it. Bud's face didn't change but his eyes gave him away.

"I...I heard you stopped one short of a thousand," I mumbled by way of explanation. "That's...um, a lot of jumps."

Bud didn't answer. In silence again we watched the first group of jumpers load up.

The Cessna took off to the south and began a circling climb to 5,000 feet. Piza's partner, whose name I didn't know, was in the plane supervising a jump for beginner students. The Twin Otter's take-off was delayed for some reason so everyone milled around and watched the 206 maneuver into position overhead. Under the tent a fat man who laughed at everything fired up a barbecue and heated coffee in a pot. Behind him one of the ladies on lawn chairs popped a Tito Fuentes tape into a boom box. The church picnic was becoming a party.

Alvaro came back.

"Mike, you'll jump from the Cessna on the third lift. Lonny will take you." – I glanced sideways at Bud who showed no reaction – "We put five people on the 206, everybody else goes on the Twin Otter. Okay?"

"Okay."

"Is this static line?" Bud asked.

Static line jumps were when a tether to the airplane pulled the rip cord as you went out the door. Free-fall was when a jumper pulled the D-ring or the lead chute himself.

"No, no," Alvaro said. "All free-fall."

"Is that bad?" I whispered to Bud, worried. He shook his head no, then explained that it was illegal in the States for a jumper to make a free-fall on his first time out of an aircraft unless two instructors accompanied him.

"Two? Why two?"

"To make sure you remember to open your chute."

"That doesn't seem like the kind of thing you would forget."

"You'd be surprised," he said.

A dot appeared overhead outside the 206. A chorus of "*Allí! Allí está!*" erupted from our crowd. More dots followed. One by one they blossomed into colorful rectangular canopies floating through the morning sky. Stray snow-white cumulus clouds drifted over the field as though jealous of the reds, blues, and yellows that for a while glided between them. The jumpers avoided the clouds and set up for their approaches, each choosing his own path to land as close as possible to our corner of the strip.

Calzada Larga was small compared to an airfield like, say, Howard or Albrook but that didn't mean it was Grandma's back yard. With runway and grass overruns and the buffer around the field the long axis was at least a mile end-to-end. The shorter axis was almost as wide. A dozen city blocks could have fit inside its perimeter. A square mile is a good-sized place, therefore, when you're floating down and trying to work your approach to a specific spot for touchdown.

With no wind to speak of, the jumpers displayed varying degrees of skill lining up for an approach. Two misjudged the glide ratio of their chutes, the distance forward they would float for every foot they descended. They turned south onto a downwind that was way too long, one that when they finally turned back would make them land at the opposite end of the field. I knew this because all around me the spectators, who had much experience in analyzing such matters, began loud armchair critiques that began with "No, no, no" and laughter about how somebody would be doing some walking. One jumper maneuvered himself directly overhead the tent and spiraled down from three thousand feet, wisely never letting himself drift too far off course. The other three came in from different angles and converged on roughly the same spot in the grass out in front of the parked vehicles.

Big Bud pointed to the nearest jumper.

"Don't steer so much," he advised. "See, he's doing it right but he makes too many corrections. See how he wobbles? Make an input and wait to see what it does. Then make another if you have to."

The first one to land was an American, one of the Army guys. At thirty feet up he had exactly the landing profile that Alvaro told me to use – feet together, knees bent, eyes on the horizon – but closing with the earth he lost his nerve and looked down. That made him flare late and he didn't slow as much as he should have. He tried to run his way onto the ground and tripped, tumbling into a rolling ball of cord and silk as the chute settled over him. The spectators roared with laughter. Piza limped over to see if the guy was alright.

The next two jumpers arrived at the same time. One was another beginner, this one a Panamanian about twenty years old. He flared too high and held his legs out in front of him. The parachute canopy, which is really just a wing, stalled at twelve feet and collapsed, dropping its load like a too-heavy weight. We all cringed as the youth landed heavily on his butt in the grass. My own lower back suffered a spasm of sympathetic pain as I envisaged the guy crippled for life. Bud actually swore.

But the jumper rolled over and waved that he was alright. In pain, but alright.

The jumpmaster was next. Piza's friend, a sour-faced university student with a Che Guevara beard and a Gypsy Kings t-shirt, raced in using a smaller sport chute than those the students were jumping with. He worked his approach to come in from the north and converted all his final altitude into forward speed. The effect was impressive, if dangerous. Dropping to only a few feet off the ground but moving forward at thirty miles per hour, he sustained that altitude and sped from one end of the viewing area to the other, flaring the canopy to keep his position and slowing down only gradually. He actually had to lift his feet to avoid snagging on the young Panamanian's parachute as it settled to the ground. The crowd of onlookers and his fellow club members shouted their approval.

Bud shook his head.

The last three jumpers landed varying distances away. Alvaro climbed onto the hood of his car with a pair of binoculars. Two stood up and waved that they were alright. The third one lay on the ground in a crumpled heap so Alvaro drove out in his Montero to investigate. He returned with all three jumpers, one of whom had a twisted ankle. That was two injuries, I thought. Two out of six.

We watched the second lift go up. The Twin Otter went first, taking a huge load of the Panamanians and more of the Army guys. The 206 carried less experienced people and it took them longer to load up, but they were also jumping from a lower altitude. The result was that both airplanes – apparently not talking to each other – reached their jump altitudes at the same time. This time the sky was filled with dots that converged on each other as the higher jumpers came down from 9000 feet to meet up with those who had jumped at five. I saw Bud cringe. But the big sky-little airplane theory must apply to people, too, because soon thirty canopies of every color popped out all over.

The crowd under the tent cheered.

As they descended, again some jumpers calculated wrong and went wide in their pattern. Most, however, converged on the area by the cars.

"This ought to be interesting," Bud mused.

It was. So many chutes came in from so many directions that the jumpers eyed each other as much as they did the ground. For all that, only a few were smart enough to maneuver to the far side of the runway and accept a hundred-yard walk. The rest poured in in a multi-sided game of chicken.

"*Puta!*" one of them yelled as he started his flare just opposite the barbecue only to have a club-mate smash into his canopy from above. The latter's feet caught in the risers, tripping up his own landing and causing the first jumper's chute to collapse. Fortunately he was only a few feet above the ground at the time but he still landed like a sack of potatoes. It wounded his pride if not his body. He came up cursing.

Another jumper made a butt landing. This time it was a Panamanian who tried to get close to the crowd but at the last second realized the danger and turned hard right. His legs swung out at the bottom of the pendulum and he didn't get them under him again in time. He yelped in pain when he hit.

"*Oye! Qué haces?*" was the next cry.

It was directed at three jumpers who overshot the zone and went into the parking area. They had to overshoot to avoid landing on the others below them but now that put them amongst two dozen cars with no altitude to maneuver. I watched one clip my radio antenna and then crash into the Montero behind me. Another scraped across the hood of a Porsche 944, causing the owner – still 60 feet in the air – to scream bloody murder and change his own trajectory at the last second so that he could land closer to the offender and beat hell out of him. The last of the parking lot trio missed all the cars but went long into the kuna grass and swamp behind.

Finally they were all down. The casualty count on this jump was one compressed vertebra – the Nicaraguan doctor loaded the butt-lander into his SUV for a drive to the hospital – two more twisted ankles, a scratched face on the guy who landed in the kuna grass, and an ugly black eye suffered when one jumper landed on another.

"Okay! Third lift!" Lonny yelled as though nothing had happened.

Bud's jaw dropped.

Alvaro hobbled over.

"Miguel! Your turn now!"

I swung the chute onto my back and queried Bud once again. What did he think?

He pulled me aside.

"They're fools," he said bluntly. "Fools."

"Should I jump?"

"It's up to you."

"I want to jump." I really did. Even with all the buffoonery around me I wanted to experience what it was like.

Bud understood. "Then jump. They're dumbasses but the equipment's alright. As long as you use it the way you're supposed to you'll be fine."

"What if I freak out going through the door and can't remember anything I'm supposed to do?"

Alvaro walked up as I said that. He frowned and patted the pager-like device he just now strapped to the front of my chute.

"You won't forget. You're smart. You're too smart for that. But when you do, this will open the parachute for you. This will open for you."

I wasn't so sure about being smart but noticed he said "when" I forgot rather than "if."

"What's that?"

"It's an AOD," Bud explained. "An automatic opening device."

I looked at the crowd of more experienced jumpers waiting for the Twin Otter.

"They're not wearing any," I mumbled, wondering if I looked like the geek at school.

Bud followed my gaze. "Don't underestimate the stupidity of people in large groups," he replied. "What altitude?" he asked Alvaro.

"Two thousand feet," Alvaro told him.

"Make it three thousand."

Alvaro hesitated but made the adjustment.

"Why three thousand?" I asked.

Bud shrugged. "You in a hurry? It gives you more time in case you have trouble."

"Thanks for the warm fuzzy."

"You'll be fine."

"If I land like that last guy Rasmussen will kill me."

"Then don't land like that. And don't land here! You've got a hundred football fields out there. Land in one of them."

Along with the AOD was a small transmitter tied to the left shoulder strap. It was a one-way radio that looked as technologically advanced as the walkie-talkies I had played with as a kid. Three other jumpers in my round had them. All of us were Alvaro's students and all of us were making our first jump. He wanted to be able to guide us from the ground as soon as our parachutes opened. As mentioned, he worried a lot.

Lonny rounded up one more student and herded all of us onto the 206. The Twin Otter was ready now, too, so the more experienced club members grabbed their equipment and lined up to pack inside it. With them went four of the soldiers from Fort Clayton. Today they would leap from 8000 feet while we in the Cessna went out at five.

"Mike! You're tallest. You get in first."

The Cessna 206 is a great plane but it isn't big. With six jumpers and a pilot on board ours was packed. The door on the right side had been removed so a gaping hole was there under the wing for whoever was unlucky enough to sit beside it. I squeezed into the spot where the co-pilot's seat should have been. My head and helmet were jammed under the panel and my legs were a cushion for the next student. The pilot, a skinny local dude in his twenties named Roland, observed my discomfort and shrugged to indicate there was nothing he could do about it.

Besides me on the plane there was Lonny, two Army soldiers in their late teens, the younger brother of the Panamanian kid who'd landed on his butt, and a local girl of about eighteen. She was the girlfriend of one of the Army guys on the Otter and was jumping because he and others in the crowd had dared her. Lonny selected her to go first, which meant she had to sit next to him by the open door during the long climb to altitude. Before we loaded she vomited in the grass from nervousness.

"She'll back out," Roland muttered.

But the girl didn't. She drank some water and insisted on going. I was impressed. When the engine started up I had a panic attack myself and would have gotten out if I could have unlocked my legs.

We took off to the south and climbed into the mid-morning air that was still fresh and clean with the fragrance of a new day. More white puffy clouds formed at three to five thousand feet, enough that Roland maneuvered around them as we ascended, but there was nothing that threatened bad weather. Whenever he banked left I could see past his shoulder and glimpse the bright blue outside. Otherwise I was confined to staring at his right leg and the back side of the instrument panel where a jumbled confluence of wires and cannon plugs gave me no confidence in his gauges.

My helmet cushioned the vibrations of the engine only a few feet from my head but I could hear Lonny shout instructions. He did that a lot, which is how I knew I wasn't the only one having second thoughts.

When we reached five thousand feet Roland lined up on Calzada Larga and called a one-minute warning. Depending on how quickly we could move, he and Lonny intended for all of us to go out on the first pass. The butterflies in my stomach grabbed baseball bats and started swinging. Evangelina, the girl in the door, began to cry.

Lonny leaned over her to look outside and give last-minute corrections to Roland.

"*Recto!*" he cried, his voice coming to us over the roar of the engine and the wind. "*Derecha! Derecha! Más a la derecha! Rectoooo!*"

Roland flew looking over his shoulder to see Lonny's hand signals. He did a textbook job of keeping his scan inside and outside the plane, watching for traffic and monitoring the gauges at the same time. Not a bad job to have, I thought, trying to keep my mind off what was coming next.

"*Ya!*" Lonny shouted.

We were overhead. Roland pulled the throttle back to minimize the windspeed as we jumped. I tensed to move.

But Evangelina wasn't going anywhere. She froze in the door and locked a rock-climber's grip on a floor stanchion. Sobbing loud enough that I could hear her, she said she had changed her mind and wanted to go back down.

Lonny talked to her, trying to convince her to change her mind again. The problem was that she was in the door and the interior of the cabin wasn't big enough for any of us to shift positions. Heck, my left foot had gone to sleep five minutes after take-off and I wasn't sure I would be able to move it even after all the others jumped out. If she didn't go, none of us did.

Other than hearing his frustration I couldn't make out what Lonny was saying. But whatever it was, Evangelina wasn't buying it.

Finally Roland throttled up and banked toward a downwind heading. A frightened jumper didn't surprise him. He had seen them before and so prepared to make a few passes to give Lonny time to work his soothing magic.

On the second time around Evangelina still wouldn't jump. Her panic became contagious.

The Army guys exchanged glances that suggested they wouldn't mind going back down, either. I began to sympathize with her plight. What did she see out the door that I couldn't? Maybe she was the only one of us with common sense. *You go, girl!* I found myself thinking.

On the third pass Lonny was still talking and Evangelina was still saying no, though not as hysterically as earlier. I began to tire of the routine. My butterflies were bewildered.

Lonny must have felt the same way. As we neared the end of the approach track, with Evangelina's voice still rising above the wind saying "*No, no, Dios mío, no,*" there was a sudden yelp...and she was gone! A long wail signaled her departure.

He pushed her, I thought. He actually pushed her.

Roland looked over his shoulder in alarm. He hadn't expected Evangelina to go. Whatever look he got back from Lonny didn't clear the confusion. Everyone who could leaned forward to look out the door and watch Evangelina's descent.

We banked around for another holding pattern since there wasn't time on our current track for the rest of us to jump. This time I could see Lonny as he leaned out the door and gave the pilot hand signals. The slipstream caught his face, blowing his hair back and inflating his cheeks whenever he opened his mouth to speak. He looked like a bulldog in the back of a speeding pickup.

"*Más a la izquierda! Rectoooo!*"

When we came upwind the fourth time none of us remaining students – having seen a girl lead the way – delayed any more than normal panic demanded. The two Fort Clayton boys went first, then Sore Butt's brother. I slid across the floor of the plane as fast as I could. Lonny held up a hand, delaying me for spacing. Then it was my turn.

I looked down and immediately regretted it. The ground was so far away my eyes had nothing to latch onto. Vertigo hit me like a linebacker.

"*Listo?*" Lonny shouted.

I swayed in the door. My stomach did somersaults. I began to hyperventilate.

"*Listo?*" he repeated.

I looked down again. *Ready?* For what, to die? What the hell was I thinking? And why hadn't five thousand feet ever seemed so high before? The world and its sky stretched out before me, impossibly big. I pulled inside and turned my head into the wind instead of down. We were only a mile up but I could have been in outer space for as far away as the ground looked.

"Move up! Farther up!" Lonny screamed in my ear.

I slid forward another inch. It was only seconds since the last jumper had gone but it seemed like hours. Our upwind leg carried us over the north end of the drop zone with the plane plowing through the air at a mile a minute. The slipstream grabbed at my legs and shoved them back toward the tail of the plane. It occurred to me I had never been shown how to jump. Alvaro had showed me how to land, he showed me how to arch in the air, but he never showed me how to get out of the damned plane! I had imagined getting in the door with no trouble: left foot on the tiny step, left hand forward, right leg hanging nonchalantly down in preparation for launch. On the grass it looked easy. On the grass there was no sixty-mile-per-hour wind. Here there was wind and there sure as hell was no grass, at least not for five thousand feet. With every move I made the slipstream threatened to knock me off-balance and out the door. I'd never been so scared in my life.

"Remember!" Lonny yelled. "Count to ten and then pull! JUMP!"

I couldn't. There was no way.

"*JUMP!*"

"I don't..." I started to say.

"*JUMP!*"

I jumped.

In the park, Alvaro had instructed me to yell 'Arch!' whenever I leaped off the garbage can.

That was to remind me to adopt the correct free-fall position as soon as I left the plane: arms and legs outstretched, head thrown back, pelvis thrust forward so my body would be curved and aerodynamic. He also wanted me to repeat the mantra of DROP-SET-CHECK-CONFIRM-PULL-WAIT so I would be sure to follow the correct procedures in getting the chute out. Lonny's technique of counting was a new one. If I had bothered to say all that crap after going out the door, I would have been a hood ornament on somebody's Land Cruiser before I finished.

Here's what I yelled instead:

"AAAAAAUUUUUUUGGGGGGHHHHH-HHH!"

I tried to arch but in half a second all I saw was sky-ground-sky-ground-sky.... I threw my arms out but the wind flipped me over like a quarter at the start of a football game. In a panic I began to flail. It occurred to me in a flash that all the garbage cans in the world can't prepare your body for what it feels like to fall. There is no sensation like it. The helplessness, the uncontrollability, the pure unnatural act of dropping like a frozen turkey threw my gyros and nerves for a loop. The farthest distance I had ever fallen before was twelve feet from a diving board – today I fell twelve feet before I even started yelling. My brain had no collective memory to draw on. As the controlling agent of my body it threw up its hands and walked away.

I was supposed to pull out the lead chute at 3,500 feet and let it go. The problem was that the altimeter on which I was to read 3,500 feet was strapped to my left wrist like an oversized watch – I couldn't stop flailing long enough to see the needle.

Then training kicked in.

Instead of throwing my hands back up I brought the left one down in front of my face, palm outward. My right hand shot down to grab the lead chute from its little pocket at the bottom of the pack. I was still tumbling, not stable like I was supposed to be, and I didn't know what altitude I was at. Maybe it was too soon? Hell, maybe it was too late. At the moment I wanted more than anything else to stop falling and there were only two ways that was going to happen. I grabbed the lead chute in my hand, held it straight out to my side, and let go.

For a few seconds nothing happened. There was the sound of cloth fluttering and that was all.

Crap.

Then, still tumbling, I felt as well as heard the main chute go out. Fabric whistled by my head going straight up. A second later...*WHAM!* The main canopy opened and jerked me to a halt.

Not actually to a halt. I still fell but compared to the 100+ mph I had just been doing the sedate descent that started when the parachute opened felt like nature had applied full brakes.

The initial opening yanked me backwards and up. My legs swung out in front of me.

The next step was to check the canopy but I couldn't do that because I couldn't raise my head. With all my tumbling the lines had twisted down to the harness, keeping me from raising my head and choking me for air. The chute was partially collapsed. In panic I realized I was descending too fast.

Desperately I reached up to grab the risers and pull them apart. At the same time I kicked in a bicycle motion as Alvaro had instructed. At first nothing happened. Then slowly I began to spin to the left. Round and round and round. The world below turned like a green 45 rpm record. Then there was another jerk as the lines untangled. The world stopped spinning. Looking up I experienced the tremendous relief of seeing a full canopy. Looking down I experienced even greater relief in seeing the ground a long way away. I had pulled too soon after all.

"Bueno, bueno. Número uno, escúcheme..." crackled the radio on my chest.

I looked down again. Four parachutes at various altitudes below me were maneuvering to the landing zone. Apparently we had all panicked and opened high because even Evangelina was just now getting close to the ground. On the one-way radio Alvaro's Spanish became pleading.

"Jumper number one, listen to me now. Evangelina, bring your feet together. That's it. No, no, bring them together. Evangelina, don't look down. You're looking down, princesa. Keep your feet together and bend your knees. Jumper number one, bend, bend, beeeennnnd,... you're not bending, querida! Get ready to land now. Eyes on the horizon and don't flare high...eyes on the horizon...that's it...that's it...no, no, bend your knees. Don't flare yet! Don't flare..."

Silence. Below me Evangelina's red and white canopy sank into the grass.

A sigh.

"Bueno, Jumper number two..."

My position overhead the field was perfect. Lonny had jumped me just past the parking area so all I had to do in order to land near the tent was not stray too far. In fact, with a slight pull on the left riser I would land a hundred yards south of the tent which was what Bud wanted. While Alvaro talked the next three jumpers down I got my breathing under control and paused to look around.

There was nowhere else like this in the world. Only a couple of thousand feet up from the surface the sense of being out in the boondocks disappeared. The canal was *right there!* It lay close by to the west, close enough that I reached out a hand to grasp it. It flowed into Lago Gatún whose immense size was only now to manageable scale. I could see the lake, the dam, the patch of green beside the dam that was a squadron drop zone, and farther still Fort Sherman and the city of Colón. Beyond it all was the Atlantic Ocean. Only fifteen miles away it was a vast dark-blue oval that perfectly divided the lighter sky from the deep green earth. And behind me, could I really see...

FOUR-LINE, STEER, CLEAR...

I realized I hadn't finished Alvaro's checklist. Reaching up I found the toggles for the cutaway panels that would give me greater forward speed and better maneuverability. Carefully I pulled down. With a jolt that gave me near heart failure, four rear panels overhead gave way. The canopy dipped. An increase in the rush of air past my helmet told me we were suddenly moving faster. I watched my feet race across the air park below with surreal speed. Between them and the ground two seagulls flew past me in the opposite direction. Seagulls! Flying below me! I laughed out loud.

With a tug on the right riser I curved around to the south.

The scene in this direction was equally dramatic. There was Panama City, the towers of

Punta Paitilla pointing up like bumps on a continent-size Braille card. The vast Pacific Ocean lay beyond them. I turned another ninety degrees to get the view that was a once-in-a-lifetime shot. Both oceans in plain sight, filling my peripheral vision as I looked east or west, spreading out to each horizon with power and majesty that made me feel infinitesimally small. And yet, having both of them there, knowing that I could see them like this only because I'd had the courage to leap from a plane made them somehow my creation. I shouted in delight. It was the most stunning thing I had felt in my life.

I landed just as I had in the park: feet first then a roll. It was as graceful as a fat man tripping.

Alvaro was helping the previous jumpers but Big Bud was there before I could get to my feet. For the first time all day – for the first time since I had known him – he didn't look pensive. He saw the look on my face as I descended and knew exactly where it came from. In his eyes was a spark I had not seen before. He looked happy.

"Yeah?" he said expectantly.

I lay in the grass looking up, my skin still feeling the air rush past me from toe to head. The sky was *sooooooooo* big above us. I lay there dizzy in a reverse vertigo trying to take it all in. The ground against my back felt good.

"Oh-ho-ho-ho, yeah!" I replied. "Oh, YEAH!"

He helped me to my feet. I started babbling. I told him about the jump, the fall, the world, the oceans, the canal, the little plane getting smaller and smaller as it flew away, the ground, the air, the sky, the birds, the buildings, the grass, the trees, the lake. My apartment! I could see my apartment! The words ran together with all the superlatives I could think of. Bud let me jabber and listened with a smile. For a few minutes all was right in our world.

We gathered up the parachute that deflated beside me in the tired breeze. I was just encouraging him to join me on another jump when we heard Evangelina scream, then several screams.

"*Ay, pobrecito!*"

We looked around, then up. At three hundred feet one of the jumpers from the Twin Otter was hurtling toward the earth face up, flailing uselessly at the tangled straps around him.

No, was my only thought. *No*.

It was six months later that Bud's PJs rolled into town. They were there for Exercise Fitful Wind, an annual training event in Honduras, but more broadly their purpose was to re-start the regular rotations that had stopped with the call-up for the Persian Gulf war. There were eight of them, two teams of four divided between the specialties. Grateful to escape the overcast winter at McChord AFB outside Seattle, they re-claimed their home in Hangar 2 and geared up for work.

But soon they had a problem when a vacancy appeared in one of their teams. The vacancy came about because the Assistant Secretary of Defense for Procurement, a Mr. W. Spencer Jarvis, visited Howard as part of a Gulf War sweep to ensure the armed forces in the rest of the world had not depleted their essential war materiel because of the Middle East campaign. A retinue of staffers accompanied Mr Jarvis. Brigadier General Heidl, our wing commander, ordered that each squadron and tenant unit prepare to host a visit by the "Assistant Sec-Def."

The PJs had just shown up but their NCO in charge, a crusty master sergeant named Wolverson, seized the opportunity to make a point. He staked out a corner of our hangar and laid out the oldest, most beaten-down equipment his team had brought along. Paint-flecked scuba tanks, rebuilt regulators, wet suits with patched holes and dive masks that were scratchy; frayed and dirty fast-ropes; a re-sewn rappelling harness; and a RHIB (Rigid Hull Inflatable Boat) that looked like it had been bought at auction. Some spots he left empty, substituting instead hand-drawn signs that said "Out of Stock," "On order – awaiting funds," or "Request for Replacement Parts Denied." Then MSgt Wolverson pressed his uniform, polished his boots, and awaited the VIPs.

The visit wasn't long in coming. Neither was the reaction to it. As it happened, Mr. Jarvis had a brother-in-law who had been picked up in Vietnam by Jolly Greens after ejecting from the back seat of an F-4. He walked thoughtfully past Wolverson's display, asking pointed questions, his smile turning tightlipped and the furrows in his brow rolling together. Behind him the line of generals and colonels twisted uneasily as he walked, a confused slinky. Finally the Asst. SecDef stopped.

"Sergeant, this disturbs me," he grumbled. He was a large man with a double chin that made it look like his face rested permanently on his chest. When he smiled he looked forward. When he frowned his gaze dropped. Now pensive, his eyes had a downward cast as though seeking a solution amidst the woebegone stack of equipment.

"Sir?" MSgt Wolverson asked innocently. Red beret firmly in place, he didn't look crusty for once. Instead he projected the image of a reliable, determined professional who made do with what he had and expected no more.

Mr. Jarvis pointed at the RHIB.

"Do you feel comfortable going to sea in that?" he growled, the voice resonating against his sternum.

MSgt Wolverson nodded in thought.

"I see what you mean, sir. No, sir, I don't. But we do what we can with what we've got." Steely eyes, firm jaw. The resolute warrior. Somewhere angels wept.

"But surely you can get replacement parts?" Jarvis challenged. He stopped before a backpack radio sitting alone on the concrete. A picture taped to the folding antenna showed a combat controller on one knee in a field, directing fire from unseen aircraft. An attached note said "Lithium batteries discontinued – replacements not available."

"Sometimes, sir," Wolverson sighed. "Sometimes not. Parts cost money and" – another sigh – "often money is hard to come by."

Mr. Jarvis' scowl deepened. His gaze sank lower. You could have hidden a puppy between his chins. He turned to look at the general behind him, who shrank away and turned to the general behind him, who whirled to the colonel beside him, who spun to the lieutenant colonel behind him. The lieutenant colonel twisted to his next in line, and so on down through two more O-5s, three majors, a captain, two senior master sergeants, and an Airman First Class until reaching the last person in line, a civilian secretary named Adam who carried a leatherbound notepad. Adam glanced behind him, saw no one, and so looked back at the A1C and shrugged. The A1C turned forward and shrugged. The senior master sergeant did the same. The shrug worked its way back to the front of the line until reaching the general, who caught himself just in time and realized one doesn't shrug to an assistant secretary of defense. He substituted a sympathetic nod, confirming for Mr. Jarvis that indeed money is often hard to come by.

There was an awkward silence.

"Yours is an important profession, Sergeant," Mr. Jarvis said slowly.

MSgt Wolverson was modest.

"We like to think so, sir. Of course, other units have needs, too, and we understand that."

The angels, already weeping, started bawling.

Jarvis continued. "My brother-in-law was saved by a PJ in '72. He told me once it was the most comforting feeling for an airman to know that wherever he was, if he was in trouble, his Air Force would come for him."

"Yes, sir. That's our motto. 'That Others Might Live.'"

"I believe," Jarvis grumbled, turning his head again – the slinky poised to react – "I believe that we have funds set aside for special cases like this. Isn't that right, General?"

The two-star turned to the one-star. "We have money for cases like this?" he repeated. The one-star turned to the O-6. "We have money for cases like this?" And so on and so on, down the line. It was like watching dominoes pivot instead of fall. The question reached back to Adam. Adam consulted his leather binder and said, "Yes."

"Yes," said the airman first class.

"Yes," said the senior master sergeant.

"Yes," said the captain.

"Yes," said the major.

"Yes," said the lieutenant colonel.

"Yes," said the bird.

"Yes," said the one-star.

The two-star took a deep breath as though considering the issue.

"Yes," he said to Mr. Jarvis.

Mr. Jarvis thought some more. "How much," he finally asked, "do you think it would cost to get your unit the kind of equipment it needs, Sergeant Wolverson? I don't mean just mission-capable but fully up-to-speed. The kind of pararescue unit the Air Force expects to have at its fingertips. The kind that gets there when all other hope is lost. The kind that brings our people home. I think that's what our young men and women over in the Gulf right now want and deserve to know is waiting in the wings for them should they ever need it. How much money would that take?"

A sheet of paper materialized in MSgt Wolverson's outstretched hand. Nobody saw him even go for a pocket.

"$1,242,718.30," he replied without blinking an eye. "Of course, that includes the newer carbon filters on the re-breathers which aren't standard issue yet but they will be by next year, and that also includes the GAU-5s instead of the A-1 model M-16 – which would actually be cheaper if you went to the right supplier. I could knock those down but the RHIBs still aren't cheap. A realistic figure could be rounded to one-and-a-quarter million."

Holding the gaze of a deserving schoolboy he passed over the itemized list.

Mr. Jarvis took the list and asked the question.

"General, do we have one-and-a-quarter million dollars?"

"Do we have one-and-a-quarter million dollars?"
"Do we have one-and-a-quarter million dollars?"
"Do we have one-and-a-quarter million dollars?"
"Do we have one-and-a-quarter million dollars?"
"Do we have one-and-a-quarter million dollars?"
"Do we have one-and-a-quarter million dollars?"
"Do we have one-and-a-quarter million dollars?"

Adam checked his book.

"Yes."

"Yes."

"Yes."

"Yes."

"Yes."

"Yes."

"Yes."

"Yes."

The general cleared his throat.

"Yes."

And so in the space of thirty minutes Wolverson's PJs became the best supplied pararescuemen in the Air Force. His men loved him.

Brigadier General Heidl hated him. He saw through the performance the instant he heard about it and demanded Wolverson's head on a plate, mixing his biblical metaphors somewhat by calling him a "Judas in uniform." Fortunately, Wolverson's team leader wasn't as familiar with the Bible as the general and besides was one step ahead of him. He put his favorite master sergeant on the first plane headed north and got him safely off base and out of the country.

But with Fitful Wind coming up that left one of his teams a man short.

The Army guy getting killed really freaked out Bud. Hell, it freaked me out, too, but I didn't have a background of demons waiting to pounce. Here he'd taken the huge step of going to the drop zone with me – re-living memories, getting the old juices flowing, getting psyched up to fill the one void in his life – when Fate suddenly appeared to slap him down and remind him in the most grisly, brutal fashion just what might lie in store should he tempt it once again. Worse, he felt responsible. Not fully, but in part. He *saw* the buffoonery, the lack of training, the flawed equipment – why hadn't he said something? At least to the Americans. He could have stopped that jump. Which of course was a foolish thought, an unnecessary flogging of his own soul, but Big Bud had it again and again and again. When he woke up in the morning now, each day it was on the side of a mountain in Colorado, looking at the sky and wondering why he wasn't dead. For a while Walt took him off the flying schedule. Lt Col Rasmussen quietly asked the chaplain to speak to Bud. I didn't know what to say. At the time I thought he would have a breakdown. On the way home from Calzada Larga he cried.

So months later when Capt Wade Bolrok walked into the squadron asking who was jump-qualified it didn't surprise me that Bud didn't raise his hand. But Wade already knew the answer and tried to convince Rasmussen to loan Bud to him for a while.

"It's a water jump," the team leader explained. "Off the coast about a mile. We'll swim in, secure the LZ, and mark it for your aircraft. McIlhenny could do it in his sleep. We know he can swim and he's got a million jumps under his belt."

"Why can't you do it with three guys?" Lt Col Rasmussen asked.

"We can," replied the team leader. "But we won't meet the deadlines the plan calls for. Without Wolverson I have to shift his equipment to the rest of the team and spend more time setting up the zone. I need a guy to get to the far end of the strip as fast as possible and clear the aircraft in. We fall a man short and it'll shift the whole exercise to the right at least twenty minutes. All he has to do is jump, swim, and run. I've seen his record. It's a triathlon he could do naked."

"Where's your other team?"

"They're doing a jump the same night at Golosan. Fifty miles down the coast. The idea is to prep two fields for simultaneous hits."

"You going to do a train-up? A practice jump or five?"

"Absolutely, sir."

Rasmussen considered it. On the one hand it was stupid to have an aircrew member do anything other than aircrew duties. You don't pound nails with a crescent wrench, as my dad used to say – at least, not if you have a hammer available. If

Bud got hurt it would take some explaining to the Air Force why a pilot was out playing Rambo. On the other hand, Rasmussen knew Bud had vast parachuting experience, swam a mile a day, and had worked with the PJs enough to make his own decision. Rasmussen also liked having people in his squadron who could do different things. He liked the oddballs. He figured it was prudent to keep a square peg around a field of round holes under the theory that you never knew when a square hole might come along. If you could convince him to hoard enough square pegs sometimes outlandish ideas weren't so far-fetched.

Sometimes.

"Lt McIlhenny, can you think of any reason in the world why it's a good idea to let you jump with the PJs?"

Bud stood in the commander's office staring hard at a picture on the wall. The photo was of a Casa 212 upended in a muddy field, one wheel dug sideways into an irrigation ditch and a wingtip resting in the furrows. His eyes burrowed into the photo as he shut out the discussion in the room, concentrating on the picture as though he could force the plane back onto firm ground through sheer will.

Lt Col Rasmussen walked over and tapped the picture.

"Never get in a cockpit with someone braver than you," he summarized. "Well?"

Bud shifted his gaze to the floor.

"No, sir," he answered. "Not a one."

"Neither can I," Rasmussen decided. This one time he had enough square pegs. "Sorry, Wade," he told the PJ. "You'll have to go with three."

We moved most of the squadron up to central Honduras for the exercise, to the air base at Soto Cano with its desert landscape and wood plank cabins in lieu of dormitories or tents. Soto Cano was a comfortable airfield but it sat in an arid valley with little population nearby. When we weren't flying there was nothing to do but sit on the hooch steps and watch tumbleweeds blow by.

Fitful Wind would take place mostly on the north coast. The Army, in the form of Task Force Bravo, would train itself and Honduran infantry in overland movement, search and recon, and direct-action missions against simulated enemy strongholds. There was also a company of Rangers down from Georgia. The Navy, in the form of a handful of special-boat operators, was training the Hondurans in coastal patrol and interdiction on the numerous rivers accessible from the ocean. The Air Force had two players: the C-27s were there to airdrop everybody and to provide a platform for airstrip assaults; the PJs were there for on-scene medical support and to mark the strips for assaulting.

Charlie Manson and Mike Vaneya were our exercise planners. They set up shop in the first hooch next to the chapel and set about determining what our missions would be and who would fly them.

I was crewed with Manny. Tony Clovella was our loadmaster. Tony was our squadron Hawaiian. I say "our" Hawaiian because he was the only C-27 guy who came from Hawaii, except that he didn't. He was from Samoa but worried that us calling him "our Samoan" sounded too much like a homosexual code.

The three of us got along well despite never having flown together before. Manny was in command. The missions were easy, a lot of airdrops. We had four C-27s up for the exercise and for the first week every one of them flew every day. For a while the troops just wanted "elevators" where instead of flying a mission profile to the drop zone we would just load up everyone at the field, take-off and circle overhead, then have them jump out. Then we would circle down and land to do it all over again. It was almost no training for us but we put up with it because we knew that however bored we were, it was riskier for the guys going out the door.

And if nothing else it let Tony work on his personal skills. Though our stereotype of a Samoan was a large, affable guy, Tony was short and skinny and obsessed by both those things. He worked out like a fiend and with Major Harmon's help had bulked up fifteen pounds over the summer. Unfortunately, he couldn't do anything about being five-foot-two. None of us cared – our short-guy jokes were reserved for Little Bud Blair. But particularly when we worked with Rangers or special teams from the Army or Navy, where size and strength were big credibility factors, Tony became insecure. Insecurity fed frustration and frustration made him aggressive. So when, prior to every jump, the twenty-or-so troops gathered around the ramp of the aircraft for a quick procedures brief, Tony had his few moments to make sure they knew who was in charge. He would vault up onto the ramp and whistle for attention.

"ALRIGHT, LISTEN UP! I'm Sergeant Clovella and I'm your loadmaster on this jump! That's right – YOUR loadmaster. I'm the guy who's going to sit you down, stand you up, move you along, and kick you out! This one is aircrew-directed so you don't have a jump master" – which wasn't actually true; the jumpmaster was always there but on pilot-directed jumps he monitored rather than directed the "go" order – "so you do exactly what I tell you to. YOU GOT THAT?! *Exactly* what I tell you!"

At this point Tony would glare around his audience to seek out dissenters. A few would chuckle but nobody mouthed off. The idea that these huge guys who lived in the mud and humped twenty miles wearing heavy packs were going to be ordered around by a pallet-pushing, hotel-sleeping Air Force guy – and a small one at that – was laughable. But the Army was always good about working with the Air Force: they nodded and smiled and said "hooah, sir" and then did whatever they wanted anyway.

In Tony's favor, he made points by trying. Ground-pounders never respect aircrew but they still want to believe we know what we're doing. Tony gave them that. When he got up on the ramp and barked at them they could make jokes about his height but still be sure that he was competent and safe, that when they got on the plane he was going to order them around and tell them exactly what they should be doing and when. And Army guys, no matter how big, needed that.

All our practice jumps for this exercise were to Tamara Drop Zone, a dirt strip twenty miles southeast of the air base. The strip wasn't big but the field it sat in was. Trees bordered it on four sides in a loose rectangle and a stream cut across the northeast corner. It was a good DZ for beginners.

The first morning we flew to Tamara we took a load of Rangers. Their company commander was driving to the zone from Comayagua and was supposed to get there to observe the drop but when we arrived at 700 feet overhead he still hadn't arrived. There was only a pair of combat controllers in the zone, sitting on the tailgate of their pickup drinking coffee and eating beef jerky. They called the area clear. After consultation with the platoon leader we decided to make the drop without waiting for the commander. Manny circled back to the west for a run-in of 030 degrees. We tested the winds, tweaked the CARP (computed air release point) which was the exact spot over the earth where the jumpers would go out the door, and came up with a release point approximately one hundred yards short of the desired Point of Impact.

"Give the team a three minute call," Manny directed Sergeant Clovella.

We couldn't see him from the cockpit but back at the ramp Tony waved three fingers in the jumpmaster's face and screamed "THREE MINUTES!" above the noise of the engines. The jumpmaster spun on his heel and passed the information to his troops, along with an order to get to their feet. In response, there was a muffled "WANJAHR! WRANN UNHEUF!" Then a pounding of boots and a chorus of voices repeated the command to stand up.

I loved the Rangers. They were so uncomplicated. By means of a long, ruthless training program they went from being crude, uneducated foot-soldiers to being crude, uneducated, heavily-armed foot-soldiers who followed orders to the letter and who loved to kill people and blow things up. They also did nothing without orders. When the SEALs jumped from our aircraft they generally slept until the ramp was open, then casually gathered their gear and charged into the blue when given the signal. The Rangers, on the other hand, looked to their platoon leader for permission to breath.

"HWIEET TUENNN!"

On their feet, two columns – "sticks" – of Rangers repeated the barked command and pivoted toward the back of the aircraft.

"ROOWK HUNHF!"

Twenty-four men shouted as they reached up to click their static lines to the cables Tony strung from the front cabin wall to an eye-bolt at the back. The first man in each column stood just forward of the troop doors. The jump master stood between the columns abeam the doors. He would be the last man out.

"Permission to open the doors?" Tony requested.

"You're clear to open," Manny responded.

Tony, hooked to his restraining harness, lifted the troop door on first the right side, then the left. Above my head on the airdrop control panel two **DOOR UNLOCKED** lights illuminated. The doors popped inward on their hinges then slid up the wall of the cabin on parallel tracks to lock in place overhead.

I couldn't see them but could easily imagine the look on the faces of the soldiers who would be first to go out the door. There was no way to avoid a kick of anxiety when the first glimmer of sunlight appeared in the open door. Especially for a jump from less than a thousand feet. The Rangers carried no reserve parachute in case the first one didn't open: at 700 feet there would be no time to activate a second chute, anyway.

"Give the team one minute," Manny advised.

Another muffled yell from Tony. Another relay from the platoon leader. Another chorus of nervous enthusiasm from the team. Each man leaned forward in position, one hand clutching his static line overhead, one hand on the shoulder of the soldier in front of him. The goal was to get everybody out as quickly as possible – on this zone they had an 11-second window – and encouragement from behind was welcome.

"You got your point?" Manny asked me.

I twisted the ailerons a hair to the right to correct one degree. As slow as we were it took exaggerated movement of the controls to change our flight path that much. When the clearing on the ground fell below the windscreen I had to use the treeline out my right leg window and a mountain ridge on the horizon to keep the proper line-up.

"Got it."

"Thirty seconds."

Manny put his hand up to the Jump panel and activated the red CAUTION light in the cabin. When he put the second switch to JUMP the red light would go out and a green light just below it would illuminate.

I leaned forward to keep sight of the drop zone. We would give the signal the instant we hit the edge of the southern line of trees.

"Five, four, three, two, one...GREEN LIGHT!" Manny called.

"GOOOOOOOO!" came the yell from the back. On both sides of the cabin the troops surged forward, pounding feet shaking the floor of the plane and drowning out the occasional thump as the 120mph slipstream threw a trooper against the side of the empennage. When the last man in the stick cleared the door, the jumpmaster checked both sides and then threw himself out the right, just as Manny called "RED LIGHT!" and flipped the switch back to OFF. 11 seconds on the nose. The Rangers were gone.

"All clear!" Tony called to us. "Twenty-five jumpers in the air. Twenty-five chutes!"

We did three elevators uneventfully, circling back to Soto Cano to pick up more troops. It was the fourth trip, with two sticks of ten, before we had any excitement.

On that flight Manny called "green light!" and twenty troops thundered out the doors, except that the second-to-last soldier on the left somehow allowed the slack in his static line to drape over the equipment slung across his chest. When he went out the door the line caught fast in a clip on his rifle. In a split-second it snagged, then caught again hard on his radio. With eight feet of line run out he cleared the door and shot into the slipstream, then spun around and slammed hard against the side of the plane. Worse, the last soldier behind him jumped and kicked him in the face as he passed by. The soldier wasn't out completely but he was dazed. He flapped in the wind like a victim of crack-the-whip, head down and inverted, hitting again and again against the cold metal just forward of the elevator.

"*Hung jumper! Hung jumper! Left side!*" Tony yelled into his mike.

I immediately cut the #1 engine to idle and put in left rudder to slip the aircraft, both efforts to reduce the slipstream on that side of the plane.

"Slow down! Slow down!" Manny urged me. "Start a climb!" To Tony, "Is he conscious?"

The response was roaring wind in our headsets. Tony had stuck his head outside to see what he could do.

Jumpers and aircrew trained for this. It happened enough on all kinds of aircraft that a "hung jumper" was a standard emergency procedure for everyone involved in airdrops. But none of us had ever seen it for real – including, presumably, the guy currently trailing our aircraft like a dangling clothesline.

"Uh, maybe. I can't tell!"

"*Shark 14, Shark 14, I've only got 19 chutes.*" The controller on the ground was anxious but kept his voice level.

"*That's affirmative!*" Manny radioed back. "*We have two alibis, two alibis. Hung jumper.*"

An alibi was anybody who was supposed to jump who didn't. The controller on the ground said "*Roger,*" and stood by for more, rightly figuring we had our hands full.

If the soldier had been awake enough and able to give a thumb's up, Tony would have grabbed the knife in his boot and cut the static line, leaving the man to drop free and pull his own ripcord. But he wasn't, meaning we would have to reel him back in.

Tony leaped past the jumpmaster. On the wall behind the left troop door was a panel marked Emergency Reel with a steel switch that said Retract/Open. Tony flipped it to Retract. The reel was just that, a hydraulically-actuated metal sleeve around the static line cable that rolled from the back of the cabin forward when activated, taking all the expended static lines with it. In this case it worked perfectly, right up until it came abeam the troop door and jammed. Two of the line clips scraped up wire on the cable to create a golf-ball sized mess of steel wool that stopped the reel in its tracks.

Tony's cursing told us all we needed to know.

Thirty seconds went by. Thirty long seconds. We all wanted the trooper back inside the aircraft. Hanging out there, spinning in the wind, the radio or harness or static line itself could give way, dropping him while he was unconscious. Who knew if his chute would open when they did?

Tony wanted him inside more than anyone. Not bothering to fix the cable he jumped to the door, grabbed the static line in both hands, and heaved. There was only room for one person to do it and he didn't give the jumpmaster a chance to help. Hand by hand, fighting a 120mph wind, he pulled the 200lb-plus jumper with all his equipment closer to the cabin. I don't know how he did it. Adrenalin maybe, or perhaps Major Harmon's workouts did the trick. Either way he got the Ranger to the door where the jumpmaster could reach out and grab the soldier's collar to help. Together they tugged him inside the cabin, pulling so hard they all collapsed to the floor.

"Cl-clear," Tony gasped into the mike.

Manny took the controls, pushed the power up, and leveled us off above 4,000 feet. He pointed us on the shortest course to the air base and its hospital.

On the ground we fixed the emergency reel but strange things continued to happen. The soldiers were using a new version of the T-1 Charlie parachute and it was a version that had issues. Even the jumpmaster admitted that unless the silk was packed perfectly it tended to do its own thing. Also, the static line attached to the chute at the top and *side* of the bag instead of the top and *back* and for whatever reason that caused the line, a wide flat cotton fiber, to snag on their equipment more than it had before.

The soldiers themselves weren't all comfortable with the new modifications. On one pass over the zone a Ranger somehow bumped the guy in front of him and caused that soldier's pilot chute to pop out in the cabin. There was a moment of chaos as some troops frantically moved clear while others jumped on the chute to smother it before it could get caught in the slipstream and sucked out the door. In the mass tackle two more pilot chutes popped out and one came close to going out the door. Then on the next pass we had to go "cold" again, keeping everybody on board, when the jumpmaster went down the line on a routine inspection and found a soldier with a tiny tear in his parachute bag. The tear went deep – a close look revealed canopy lines had been sliced. It wasn't malicious – the soldier had accidentally done it himself trying to replace a trench knife into its sleeve – but it was scary enough that we cancelled the drop and returned to the field for all the Rangers to re-pack their chutes. Had we gone ahead with the jump it's possible the soldier would have plunged to earth with nothing but a streaming line of silk to mark his passing.

On the next jump the lead Ranger froze in the door when the green light was given. The jumpmaster yelled *Go!* and tapped him on the leg but the soldier didn't go. Maybe the wind kept him from hearing the order, maybe the tap wasn't hard enough. Jumpers don't usually look at the green light so it's possible the guy just didn't know it was time to jump. Or maybe he really froze, thinking for once how stupid it was to hurl yourself out of a perfectly good aircraft. Whatever the reason, there was enough confusion when it happened that the jumpmaster yanked the soldier out of the line, sat him down, put an armed guard on him, and threw everybody else out. We then landed in the LZ with the soldier on board. On the ground, his company commander, sergeant-major, and others were there to chew his ass and find out what went wrong.

The Army wasn't the only one using new equipment. Something we had just acquired was the jump platform, a narrow ledge with a blast shield on one side that fitted into the frame of the troop door. It was like a running board on a truck, its purpose being to allow the soldiers six more inches of airplane for them to stand on before they threw themselves out the door. It had been tested on C-130s where the soldiers determined the ledge gave them just enough extra spacing that they didn't slam against the fuselage of the plane in the first moments of their jump. That was important to a soldier, important enough that SOUTHCOM directed the design be modified for all its jump-capable aircraft. So the ledge arrived just before the Honduras exercise and the Army, finding out we had it, insisted we install it.

Merrill installed the ledge – or rather, they modified it to be installed. The way it worked was that the ledge wasn't in place until right before a jump. The loadmaster slid the door open, attached the ledge to a hinge the Merrill technicians affixed to the door frame, then rotated the whole device into position. Once in position, a cotter pin and simple pressure of the slipstream against the blast shield kept it in place. There was no way it could depart the aircraft and no way it could be removed until the cotter pin came out.

The only downside of the ledge was that it was built for a C-130, not a C-27, and the doorframes on our plane were ever-so-slightly smaller. The Merrill guys had had to cut a thin slice off the sheet metal at its base and then literally pound it into a form that worked with our door. Rasmussen didn't like it and the Merrill guys weren't thrilled but SOUTHCOM insisted. Their resident expert, a senior master sergeant on loan from Little Rock, Arkansas, made a trip to Howard AB just before the exercise and pronounced our design good-to-go. So two days into the exercise we started using the ledge.

Except sometimes we didn't. Tony, for example, hadn't used it all day today. He didn't like it and didn't trust it. But after the hung jumper incident one of the Army company commanders learned we didn't have it in place and got his commander to insist that we use it from here on out.

Every military exercise goes through phases of crawl, walk, and run. They start out slow to practice each player's part then work up to complex events piece by piece until everyone is ready for the final show. The culmination is a multi-pronged affair, a combat scenario involving many players doing different things in several locations. Together the events fulfill the objective that the exercise called for.

Fitful Wind's objective was a land-grab. It was a combined (meaning the Hondurans were involved) and joint (meaning the Army, Navy, and Air Force all had roles) exercise to seize and control a triangle of land stretching from La Ceiba to Trujillo and then inland to the town of Sava. Our squadron would be dropping PJs into the ocean the night before the main assault. The PJs would swim ashore to prep the airfields at Golosan and Trujillo. Once the airfield was secure more planes would land at each field to infiltrate troops from Task Force Bravo. At dawn a final airdrop by C-27s would put Rangers and Honduran troops on the fields at Elixir LZ, just across the Aguan River from Sava. Meanwhile, the Navy and the Honduran Riverines would patrol the Caribbean coast and the shores of the Aguan.

Charlie and Mike Vaneya had their hands full. The Army and Navy both changed their plans a lot, forcing them to react. Then one of our planes broke and the mechanics realized they had not brought the right parts to fix it. And the Hondurans briefly demanded that we move to a new hooch. Charlie at one point threw up his hands and threatened to shoot the next person who walked through the door with a request for a schedule change. Mike kept his cool throughout. He was our senior ranking guy and so had to take responsibility for everything that happened on the Air Force side of the house but he shouldered that burden with a shrug and a smile. This was a man who trolled for bullets, after all. While Charlie smoldered in sarcastic tension, Mike leaned calmly on a determination to give events a chance to play out on their own before he rushed into making a decision. Above his desk he nailed a wooden sign that said "Wait," reflecting his firm belief that most crises would handle themselves.

Fortunately, just before the exercise kicked off Lt Col Rasmussen sent up Kevin Berne from Panama to help out as a planner. Kevin was a master of organization and had the experience, the knowledge, and the affable personality to deal with the Army. He could also make a decision. When he walked into the planning hooch two days before "Hit Night" there were literally pages flying around the room in a breeze that obscured from view a task-saturated Charlie

Manson. When he walked out twelve hours later it could have passed as the conference room of a law firm. Maps were laid out in order, flight plans were collated, a flying schedule was posted, and Charlie Manson had gotten a good night's sleep. All was right with the world.

So we rolled into the exercise ready to go. Because of the circadian rhythm change of flying at night after several days of flying in mid-afternoon, Kevin put three pilots on every plane to make sure nobody became too tired to fly. And to reward himself for straightening out the planning cell he put himself on one of the crews. He would be aircraft commander on my plane, muscling Manny out and sending him to do the overwater drops.

Wade Bolrok swung by the ops center twice during the exercise to try to talk Mike Vaneya into releasing Bud to him for the water jump. Mike, of course, told him no but Wade kept dropping none-too-subtle hints to Bud that they could really use him. Wade was a good guy and his motives weren't all selfish: he knew why Bud didn't jump and he'd gotten the Oprah-esque idea that it would be therapeutic – "closure" – for Bud if they talked him into it anyway. But Bud quietly refused and started avoiding Wade instead, leaving the TV room whenever he saw him or any other PJ head for our screen door. He even asked Kevin to change his crew assignment when he learned that he would be on the plane that would drop the PJs off La Ceiba. Kevin complied and put Bud on our crew. The three of us would fly troops into Trujillo and then make the dawn Ranger drop at Elixir.

The night before kick-off it was hard to sleep. Though we all tried to shift our rest schedules in the two days before the exercise it was easier said than done. Even with blankets over the windows and the air conditioners on high, crawling into bed at three in the afternoon only gave me a two-hour nap and then hours of fitful tossing and turning. At 9pm on the night of the exercise I showed up at the ops center looking like a college student who had pulled an all-nighter. Everyone else did, too.

"Morning, sunshine," Charlie Manson growled. "You look like crap. Maybe I should fly in your place."

"Maybe you should. I might fall asleep on approach."

"I've seen you fly when you're awake. It won't make any difference."

Kevin converted one wall of the hooch break room into a map board. All of Honduras was reflected there in 1:250,000 terrain planning charts. He stood in front of it now studying the maze of multicolored lines representing the flight paths of the four C-27s as well as the two

C-130s that would be coming in later in the morning from Florida. Everyone was flying a low-level route at some point in their mission and the lines zig-zagged around the central and eastern parts of the country.

"Any conflicts?" I asked, observing the huge coffee mug in Kevin's hand and wondering if anyone flying tonight would be truly awake.

Kevin pointed at a ridgeline east of the Soto Cano valley. It cut a jagged line from just northwest of Tegucigalpa all the way to where the grasslands of the central valley pointed the way to Nicaragua, a jagged zipper of steep cliffs and valleys that we all loved to fly around. Near its midpoint was an opening that could barely be made out on the map. It was a tight gorge of switchback turns that gave the only shortcut through rather than over the mountains. Some unoriginal surveyor had named it Devil's Canyon but because that name appeared somewhere on every map of every country in the world we had changed it locally to Fluffy's Beak.

"Here," he said. "Everybody wants to go into this thing while it's still dark. Walt and your boy Declan are going out through Fluffy within ten minutes of Jem and Tommy coming back the same way."

"Jem and Tommy are flying together?" I asked in amazement. Jem had recently moved up to being an aircraft commander. He was a good flyer, as was Tommy, but they were both Pinheads. We would have to inspect their plane for hookers and beer bongs before they took off. "Whose brainchild was that?"

Kevin looked at me askance.

"Oh, sorry. Well, make Jem change his route. Or just tell everyone to make sure they're on time."

"Uh-huh. How about if I tell Walt to go around the long way?"

"He'll fly through it anyway and not tell you."

"No, he won't."

"Well, he won't be happy."

"Yeah, you're right."

"But you'll do it anyway?"

He nodded. "Gotta do something and I've only got an hour. A bad decision now is better than a good decision later."

Bud showed up. He looked like he normally did, which meant how I looked with two-hours' sleep. But he had an immaculate low-level chart drawn up, a neatly-arranged checklist, and his flight gear was in order. Sleepy or not, he was ready to fly.

Jem and Manny and their crews stepped to the aircraft first, at midnight. They would take the first two planes up for a two-hour low-level route culminating in drops over the ocean. Kevin, with me and Bud, and Walt, with Declan and Evan, would wait until two a.m. to take off. We would fly separate routes to hit a time-on-target, or TOT, of 0400 hours at the two airfields on the coast.

It was dark enough outside when we stepped from the hooch that everyone carried a flashlight just to find our way to the van. Soto Cano normally shut down at sunset and there weren't any streetlights on the base roads. One naked bulb hung over a water pump across the street from the gym. Another light came from half a mile away at the parking ramp where the Merrill guys had set up diesel-powered light carts to illuminate the aircraft so they could prep them for take-off. Nothing else interfered with our beams as they stabbed through the night. We could hear the rumble of the carts echo across the base and out into the stygian valley.

A sliver of a moon darted between clouds overhead. Stars twinkled behind it. The Comayagua Valley responded with scattered twinkles of its own, a handful from the town of Comayagua miles to the north and fewer from La Paz to the south. Everywhere else on the ground it was black, a soothing absence of light where people and animals alike slept in peace. It was refreshing, the way night is meant to be.

"Dark," Bud said simply, summarizing my thoughts.

"Uh-huh. It's kind of nice."

Kevin sniffed. "Say that in an hour when you can't see the mountains a quarter mile off the nose."

He had a point. I couldn't see the hills to the east. They were huge and only miles from the base. That realization made the blackness lose some of its sheen.

"You want the first or second leg, Bud?" I asked. The first leg would be before the sun came up. "It's all the same to me," I lied.

"I haven't landed at Trujillo," he answered. "Have you?"

"Twice."

"Then how about if you do the night assault since you already know what the field looks like. I'll do the drop."

"You got it."

Damn. So much for sleeping in the cabin.

Vince and Harry, the evil twins of the mechanic corps, were half-concealed under the cowling of the right engine when we pulled up to #106. We threw our gear onto the ramp.

"Good lord," Kevin exclaimed, walking to the base of their jackstand and looking up. "What did we do to deserve the two of you launching us out?"

Vince jumped down the ladder and winked.

"Heyya, Kevin. Just lucky, big man. Just lucky. We'll have the plane for you in just a second."

"What's the problem?"

"Oh, nothing serious. We found what might have been a leak on pre-flight. Just wrapping it up now."

"*Might* have been a leak? How does that work? It's either a leak or it isn't."

Vince was the picture of earnestness. He always was, so much so that even those of us who thought he was one of the most sincere people in the world – me included – realized he could also put a snow job over any of us and we would never know it.

"Oh, no. It could have been residual from the last flight but it was in a place we didn't expect so we took a closer look. Harry found a loose fitting that he's just tightening up."

Kevin flashed his light up under the cowling. Harry was hard at work, his fingers flying over the accessory box at the bottom of the engine, but he took a second to squint into the light and flash a confident smile.

"Not to worry, boys! Not to worry! Ol' Harry and Vince will have you on your way in no time."

"What are all those parts you've got up there?"

Pieces of metal shone through the grating of the jackstand at Harry's feet.

"What parts? Those? Nothing. Nothing at all. Pay no attention to the man behind the curtain. I'll have that done in a second."

Kevin climbed up the ladder and peered over the edge.

"You know, I don't have an airframe-and-powerplant license like you guys, but that looks an awful lot like a fuel control unit."

"Oh, it is, it is," Harry assured him, his tone and his actions a masterful display of cognitive dissonance. Pulling a fuel control but saying everything is okay is like an orthodox rabbi eating a cheeseburger but vowing, "Don't worry, it's kosher."

"You took the fuel control off?"

"Yeah," said Vince, trotting around Kevin and scrambling up the ladder. "But don't worry, we'll put it back."

In his hands he held a two-foot-long piece of braided tubing. He passed it up to Harry who, without looking, swapped it out for an identical piece from the engine.

"You took the fuel control off?" Kevin repeated, his eyes wide in disbelief. "An hour before take-off?"

"Only part of it...most of it...yeah."

"But we're putting it back. There's time."

Kevin's expression was the same he would have worn had Laura told him their infant son was really sired by an alien. Since the baby was huge, to the rest of us the idea wasn't far-fetched.

"That'll take hours," he said. In his mind's-eye he saw the exercise schedule falling apart like the house of cards it was.

Harry and Vince laughed, their voices sounding tinny under the cowling.

"Give us ten minutes!"

I walked over to stand next to Kevin, whose face shifted back to its normal waiting-for-the-other-shoe-to-drop expression. We stared at the bottom half of the two used-car salesmen for a minute.

"We've got time," I offered.

"Time?" he replied. "Time for an engine FCF? At night?"

A functional check flight for an engine only took an hour. But by regulation it wasn't allowed to be done at night since there was a decent chance the engine could fail, causing the crew to scramble for a place to land. He could see us having to wait until dawn, thereby canceling our part in the exercise entirely.

Vince's head popped clear of the cowling.

"Who said anything about an engine FCF?" he demanded.

"Removing a fuel control unit requires an FCF," Kevin stated matter-of-factly. He knew his regs.

Harry's head popped clear, his munchkin face smeared with grease.

"Ah-ha! *Removing* a fuel control unit, yes. *Repairing* a fuel control unit, no. I never took the whole thing off at once. Only some pieces, then others. *Never* was the unit completely missing from the engine." He flourished his hands to demonstrate that the rabbit, in fact, was no longer there.

Kevin pointed accusingly at Harry's feet.

"*That's* a fuel control!"

Harry's eyebrows danced.

"*That's* a regulator," he pointed for himself. "And a tapbolt. And an A-frame actuator. The fuel control consists of six separate pieces and the other three are on the engine. You see?" he tapped his nose and grinned the smile of the unscrupulous. "We're thinking! Looking out for you. Seven minutes to go!" he cried and disappeared under the cowling. But he reappeared in a second, noticing me for the first time.

"Mikey! How you doing, buddy? I didn't know you were flying this line."

"No, of course not. If you had known it was me you would have removed the whole engine and told me to fly it anyway."

Harry cackled in laughter and went back to work.

"And you would have, my boy!" his voice echoed down. "That's why we like you!"

The twins were as good as their word. By the time Kevin and I buckled into our seats, Harry and Vince were buttoning up the cowling and pushing the stand away.

"You have your crescent wrench?" I yelled out the window to Harry over the sound of the aux power plant starting up.

He searched his pockets in mock horror, then shrugged.

The Army arrived. Jerry Miner, our loadmaster, took the troops aside for a briefing before loading up. Bud hopped into the third seat and went to sleep.

We ran through the pre-start checklists. Then Kevin turned on the HF radio and we waited. HF was the long-range radio of choice for the exercise. When different players completed their tasks they would call a code word over the radio to signal they were done. All the code words for things going as planned were brands of beer. Anything not going as planned would be a woman's name. We were waiting for "Iron City."

The call came at a quarter to two. It was Tommy Goode's voice, wavering through the atmosphere from a hundred miles away, calling the ops center on Soto Cano to let the bosses know the exercise had kicked off.

"Warlock, Warlock, this is Shark 12. We are Iron City. I say again, we are Iron City."

"Good," said Kevin. "The PJ's are in the water. Let's go."

We started engines, Kevin warning Jerry to keep a careful eye on #2. Jerry kept the fire extinguisher close to hand but both engines started normally. All the gauges matched up. Harry and Vince did a victory dance off the nose.

We taxied to the darkened runway and took off to the south, dodging the lights of La Paz and aiming for a pocket of starlight above the south pass. Our route took us around Tegucigalpa, outside the radio beacon at La Cruce, then east along the Nicaraguan border. We crossed the *Cordillera Entre Rios* at about 86 degrees west and followed the Patuca River east and then north until completing the square by turning back west toward Trujillo. The flight lasted two hours.

Kevin did most of the flying while I navigated. It was an arrangement I preferred when flying low-level at night. We flew at an altitude of 300 feet above the highest obstacle within two miles of our planned route, which meant keeping a keen eye on the clock and a rapid crosscheck of the other instruments. Though I trusted Kevin implicitly there was no getting around having the warm fuzzy of watching the map myself. Against the broken cloud deck with its hint of reflected moonlight we watched mountain ridges glide by only ten seconds' flying time away. At regular intervals I counted down the time to the next turn: "3...2...1...hack" at which point Kevin would bank the aircraft and we would both punch the stopwatch on our clocks, starting the next timed leg.

Timing was everything. I never stopped marveling that ten seconds of error could get me killed. The INS was a wonderful instrument but it drifted a mile every hour without updates. At night we had few updates. The clock was our life. If we stayed on speed and on course then the math was immutable and everything worked. Where we could go wrong most spectacularly was in not watching the clock. So I watched it. Somewhere in my family's past a naval ancestor may have stood on deck late at night watching for the hourglass to drain its sand so he could turn it and avoid hitting rocks, but in terms of focus he had nothing on me.

The ground below was invisible unless a village with a light passed underneath. Every few seconds Kevin crosschecked the radar altimeter and compared it to what the barometric told him. He asked at regular intervals for heading updates or the current safe escape altitude. If we bantered at all it was quick. Bud woke up soon after take-off, finding it hard to doze when the trees were only three hundred feet away. He climbed into the third seat and backed us up on the gauges. Only the soldiers in back rested. Time and the night crawled by, two hours of concentration and hard work. It was with relief that we finally turned west inside the coast and started a climb to two thousand feet. Kevin announced ten-minutes-out, a call that Jerry relayed to the team.

"Did they decide whether the lighting was going to be Amp-1 or Amp-2?" Kevin asked as we ran our descent checklist. He referred to the LZ marking pattern that the PJs would lay out on the airstrip at Trujillo. Amp-1 was a vague C-shaped pattern of colored lights that told us where the touchdown zone was. Amp-2 gave the same information but with fewer lights, a straight 6 that was harder to read.

"They were going to try for Amp-1 but Bolrok said it would depend on how much time they had. He was still concerned about not having enough guys to set up the zone in time. If they're not ready they just won't give the signal."

The signal would be illumination of the zone three minutes before touchdown. The PJs would leave the lights up for ten seconds to give us a target to shoot for as we descended from altitude. Then they would turn the lights out and not re-illuminate them until fifteen seconds prior to our TOT, by which point we should be on short final and able to use the markings to their fullest. By the rules of the exercise, if we never saw the lights the first time we couldn't descend; if we lost sight of them before touchdown we would have to go around.

The last minute of a night assault is a stressful affair, to say the least. Without night vision goggles we were descending on faith into a featureless pit. It was like closing your eyes while driving down the street and seeing how far you could count before opening them again. I marveled not for the first time how much trust we all put in each other: the troops in the back counting on the pilots, the pilots counting on the PJs, the PJs counting on the high-school-dropouts who put together the batteries in the airfield lights.

We avoided the town of Santa Rosa de Aguan by staying south of the coast, then cut north to fly over the lagoon at the base of Punta Caxinas. We coasted out over the bay and set ourselves up on a wide arc high over the water.

"You see the field?" Kevin asked me.

"No, but I see the town," I replied.

"Too bad we're not landing in town then. The field should be going to our eight o'clock. About three thousand feet long, real narrow. Black asphalt. It's east of town."

"Uh-huh. Well, from what I see the town stops and there's nothing east of it. It's a black hole."

We turned to face the mountains, three miles out and a thousand feet up. Kevin slowed our speed and we dropped gear and flaps. We could make out a thin line of foam on the ocean breakers that marked the approximate location of the beach. Inside the beach, where the airfield was supposed to be, there was nothing.

"There!"

Suddenly, in the middle of the black hole a dozen pinhole-size lights winked on. They stitched a thin but clear C parallel to the breakers. The PJs had made it to the runway.

The C was our aimpoint. Kevin fixed his gaze on the spot and started a left turn. As we rolled out on final and dropped the flaps to full down the lights went out but Kevin stayed locked on the position.

"Give the team one minute," he advised over the intercom, then set a pitch and power setting to keep us on a steady glideslope right down to the runway. We descended into the hole.

"Eight hundred feet," I announced. "Six hundred. Five hundred."

The C-27 glided down into the void, the few references we had such as the foaming breakers and the town lights receding behind us or out to the side as we got too low to see them. There was nothing outside the cockpit but blackness and nothing inside but faith as we passed through five hundred feet. I kept my hands poised on the landing lights, ready to throw them on the instant the zone lights came on again. By that time our engine noise would give up our presence anyway so we weren't concerned about being stealthy. Besides, once on the ground the assault lights were hard to see. They were also widely spaced so we needed our own lights to keep us from driving off the runway during our landing roll.

"Four hundred feet."

Where were the zone lights? Out of the corner of my eye I saw the clock tick toward 0400. Ten seconds to go. The lights should have been on five seconds ago.

"Three hundred feet."

Kevin's hand tightened on the power levers. He was seconds away from aborting the approach.

"Go a-...." he started to say.

The zone lights came on.

They came on suddenly. Other than being offset a hundred feet to the left of our approach line they were damned close. Kevin dipped the wing and jinked left, then chopped the power levers to idle. I hit the landing lights. All of a sudden the ground was there. It was mostly trees at this end of the runway. Trees, a drainage ditch, and a rolling field that ended at a slat-wood fence that slid just below our belly. More trees on our left and right leaped into the halo of light thrown off our wings. Then we were over the asphalt and down, the first zone marker dashing past the left window.

Whuumph!

"Reverse!" Kevin called. "On the brakes!"

The second marker slid by. The lights on our wings showed an oval of the world in front of us, most of it coming into view so fast there was nothing we could do except hope that an immovable object that could hurt us – say, an African elephant or a Boeing 747 – didn't suddenly appear. It was what driving instructors call "overriding the headlights" and we continued doing it until halfway down the small strip.

"Co-pilot's controls."

I grabbed the yoke so he could move his left hand to the nosewheel steering grip. Just as we made the transfer a body came into view lying prone on the tarmac, perfectly in line with our left main gear.

"Whoa!" Kevin yelled and jinked us right. The lateral move caught everyone in the cabin off-guard. We heard soldiers – who had just gotten to their feet in preparation to charge off the ramp – topple to the floor like tenpins. The body on the ground rolled away as we jinked. As best we could tell we didn't run over whoever it was. As soon as he was clear Kevin jinked back to the left to keep us from rolling into the weeds.

In the back guys scrambled to their feet, swearing.

At the end of the runway we spun around. Jerry lowered the ramp as we did and leaped aside, pointing with a chem light to the 3 o'clock position off the plane. The thirty soldiers we carried ran off the ramp in that direction.

"Team's clear!" Jerry called, activating the Close switch on the ramp and cargo door.

"Copy, standby for take-off."

I turned off our landing lights, signaling to the ground team that we were ready to depart the way we had come. Our oval world out front disappeared. All we could see now was a faint glow above the trees from the town of Trujillo two miles away. Above the glow were stars. The beach with its bioluminescent foam was off to our right. So was the small bohio that served fried fish and coconut-rum smoothies. That's where Carl Diehrmann was, I figured. Carl had been tapped to be part of the Exercise Control Team on the ground at Trujillo, the guys who watched silently from the shadows to make sure things didn't get out of hand. Nobody ever wanted to be on the ECT – it was more fun to be part of the exercise itself – and Carl was probably hating life right now. Especially after seeing our landing.

We waited. It wasn't easy. My heart was pounding.

"Think we hit him?" Bud asked from behind us.

Kevin shrugged. "If we did we're going to hit him again."

From the end of the airstrip ahead of us a green light started flashing. Kevin pushed the power up.

"Here we go. Looking for 84 knots to rotate."

I turned the landing lights back on. Our oval world reappeared, a gravelly surface that rolled under our nose faster and faster like a treadmill in a darkened room. Kevin watched it intently while I watched our speed.

"70 knots...80...84, rotate!"

The C-27 leaped back into the air. For the last time I turned our landing lights off. We climbed out and in 30 seconds were level at two thousand feet.

"Your controls," Kevin said, fatigue in his voice.

"My controls."

I wiped sweat from my hands and felt the familiar tired relief that follows an adrenalin rush. Seeing Kevin sit back to relax I added, "We need to do that more often."

He shook his head.

We flew back to Soto Cano at top speed. The plan called for Walt and us to do a two-ship airdrop of the Rangers at Elixer. The jump time was 0545. With him coming from the north and us from the south, we would only make it if we hauled ass. Entering the Comayagua Valley we caught sight of Walt's position lights on short final and managed to land five minutes behind him. In the glare of the light carts we could see the Rangers and the Honduran jumpers lined up at the edge of the parking ramp. Someone in a flight suit ran to Walt's plane as we taxied in. I guessed it to be Mike Vaneya. We pulled alongside Walt and stopped, bringing the engines to idle but leaving everything running.

"Your turn," I slapped Bud on the back as I hopped into the cabin. He took my place in the co-pilot's seat.

Jerry lowered the ramp. The first person on was indeed Mike. He trotted through the cabin, flashed a smile at me, and jumped on the steps to the cockpit to have a shouted conversation with Kevin.

"How'd it go?"

Kevin gave a thumb's-up. "No problem."

"I hear you almost squashed a PJ."

"What was he doing on the runway?"

Mike shrugged. "They called it in. It wasn't your fault, they said so themselves. Don't worry about it."

"I won't."

"How are you on gas?"

"Skosh. We need to hustle."

Mike looked over his shoulder. The jumpers were boarding, a mix of Hondurans and Rangers, making a gaggle in the center of the cabin until Jerry pushed his way through the crowd and forced them into their seats.

"Stick to the timeline. You don't have time to re-fuel. Take it into Trujillo if you need to. Carl will get you gas there."

Kevin nodded. He was spinning numbers furiously on his whiz wheel, trying to figure out if he could make it to the drop zone and back. Mike patted him on the shoulder.

"You guys are doing great! No injuries so far, everything's been on time. The colonel's real happy."

Kevin gave his like-I-care shrug. Mike returned it and hopped back into the cabin.

"You get to fly?" he yelled to me over the engines.

"Yep, all done."

He looked at the troops getting settled in their seats.

"Wish I could go with you," he lamented. "All this hoo-ah crap is driving me nuts." He waved and ran off the back of the plane.

"Shark 14, Shark 13 on uniform."

That was Walt, calling over the secure radio.

"13, go ahead."

"Are you guys good on gas?"

"Good enough. We can't do the low-level but we don't have time for that anyway. We'll just have to drop them and go."

"That checks. We're sitting on just over three thousand. We'll be landing on fumes back here if we delay."

"Copy. You still want to lead or do you want us to take it?"

It was a stupid question and everyone, including Kevin who asked, knew it. You never give up lead in a formation. Walt certainly wouldn't. When he replied he was laughing.

"Yeah, right. We'll be ready in thirty seconds. Follow us out, give us one minute spacing all the way through the drop."

"Roger. Just asking."

"How were the winds at the field?"

"Calm."

"Then we'll stick with the CARP. See you out there."

"Jerry, you ready?"

"Waitin' on you, boss."

Jerry closed the ramp and made his way forward, the corpse of a cigarette butt hanging from his lips. Smoking wasn't allowed on our aircraft but Jerry complied only in the sense that he became more discreet.

"Then let's go. Lead's taxiing. Co-pilot, your controls."

"My controls," Bud repeated, leaning forward in his seat to see around Kevin and watch Walt's plane taxi to the runway. There was a hint of pink in the eastern sky as we started to roll. Not enough to see by but enough to know that we might make it to the drop zone before dawn broke.

On departure we climbed to two thousand feet. At first it was so dark that once airborne we could only see the lights on Walt's plane and had to rely on our instruments to see he was three miles ahead flying a direct line to Elixer. But very quickly the instruments became irrelevant. The sky in the east turned from gray to blue to a soft aqua that spread along the horizon and gave us a backdrop to silhouette his plane. On Kevin's urging Bud closed the distance to a thousand feet, close enough that the winking of Walt's position lights blended into the sky out front. As quiet as the world was at that time of the morning and with as little maneuvering as we had to do, it seemed for a long time that the lead plane wasn't moving at all, that it was hovering instead while the horizon slid sideways beyond it. Flying behind it was like chasing a two-dimensional cutout across a vast canvas. Looking over Bud's shoulder I felt myself falling victim to all kinds of visual illusions, the worst being that we were the ones floating, hanging suspended in the sky by invisible strings.

Sporadic calls came in over the radio. Everything on the coast was going well except that the second wave of troops being flown into La Ceiba had been delayed. There was confusion there between the PJs on the ground and the Task Force Bravo troops as to who controlled the field once the soldiers landed. We picked up pieces of a heated conversation between Wade Bolrok and a team sergeant whose men refused to clear the runway. Meanwhile, the formation flown by Jem and Manny circled over the water waiting for clearance to bring in the next wave. Jem occasionally came up on frequency to inquire politely, *"Hey, son, y'all got it worked out yet who's gonna be boss?"*

Halfway to Elixir we heard the call we were really listening for, the execution words "Old Style" from the Honduran Riverines ("Tailpipe Whisky") who were responsible for securing the drop zone. It came in weak over the HF radio, the Honduran radio operator struggling with the English words but repeating them three times. We were now cleared to drop on arrival.

"Good on 'em," Kevin sighed. He had worried the Riverines would be late, making us hold overhead. Now he could forget about having enough gas and concentrate on the drop.

We pushed the distant lights of San Pedro Sula off to our left side and turned east. Bud was flying in a cruise position at Walt's 7 o'clock and now shifted to trail, in a straight line a thousand feet back. Walt's plane never wavered, homing in perfectly on target. In the windscreen the reflected lights off our instruments grew fainter as they contrasted less and less with the sky outside.

"Thirty miles," Kevin announced.

A short time later Bud added softly, "Give the team five minutes."

From the cockpit's third seat I watched Jerry get to his feet at the front of the cabin and take the cigarette from his mouth. Most loadmasters bellowed the time call to team members. Jerry didn't, perhaps guessing that so much effort on his nicotine-scarred lungs would cause him to implode. Instead he held his cigarette high until all the soldiers were looking at him, then he raised his other hand, palm open and fingers outstretched. The soldiers nodded and moved aside as Jerry worked his way to the ramp. One of the American troops, closest to the door, barked orders to the others and did elaborate sign language to the Hondurans about checking their straps.

"No jumpmaster?" I asked the pilot.

"No," Kevin replied. "Aircrew-directed this time."

"Why?"

"Guess there weren't enough to go around. They're trusting us on this one."

At fifteen miles out Bud pulled the power back to take spacing. Now the instruments became important again as we slowed down and maneuvered into a trail position one mile back. Kevin started talking more, reading distance and winds off the INS and chastising Bud if he drifted left or right of the aircraft out front.

Walt brought us in from the west-southwest, down the approaches of the Aguan Valley past El Cayo and Trojas and the "big" town of Olanchito. The mountains rose up on both sides to at least six thousand feet but by now we could see them clearly. It was a quarter to six. The sky in the east grew lighter, letting the ground below awaken with a gray-green glow of its own.

Following Walt's lead we descended to a thousand feet above the valley. There we could make out farms along the river and cows bunched in the high grass. Kevin pointed out smoke rising from a few chimneys. I spun my whiz-wheel but he was faster, updating our winds and heading before I could get the pencil smudge on the plastic to line up with true north. I settled for doing the same calculations on the INS computer and verifying that he was right.

"Three minutes," Kevin announced.

Jerry waited calmly at the ramp. The troops did some shouting and then got to their feet.

"We going to make it?" I asked warily, watching the clock.

Kevin frowned at the question. "We're fine. Walt's never late."

Just before the Olanchito Pass we caught a glimpse of movement on the left side of Walt's plane. Bird, his loadmaster, raised the troop doors and took a quick look outside. He then swung the new platform into position in preparation for the jump. Kevin cleared Jerry to do the same.

The sky out front transitioned through a million shades of pink on its way to furnace orange as Jerry slid the doors up their tracks. The glow came inside as he did, throwing hot rectangles across the rear of the cabin. The rectangles mixed with the red cabin lights to create an infernal scene like boiler rooms or Victorian factory floors. The troops shuffled in place, silhouettes against the industrial backdrop. Each raised his inside hand to the static line for one more check.

"One minute."

Instinctively, I checked the safety belt strapped across my lap.

"There they go," Kevin said quietly.

A mile out front, soldiers poured out of both sides of the lead C-27. They came out as indistinguishable dark bundles trailing a string. For the first half-second they merged with the fuselage of the aircraft, then they separated and became human figures, arms and legs reaching for the sky as the static line lengthened. When it reached its limit it tore open the parachute bag each man carried. Then a new, thicker line appeared, a thicker line that became several lines with a mushroom-cap head just as the men disappeared under our nose.

It all happened in seconds. Before we realized their jump was over they were gone, floating beneath us so that the only way to see them was through the window by Bud's leg. Where men had emerged from Walt's plane now only loose static lines flapped high in the windstream, fluttering close to the horizontal stabilizer as Bird dragged them in.

"Standby!" Kevin called. "Five seconds!"

Jerry crouched like a runner between the troop doors, his right arm held high. He would slap first the lead jumper at the left door, then the lead jumper at the right. Except for those two jumpers – whose attention was fixed outside – every eye in the cabin was on him.

"Green light!"

Jerry's arm came down and hit one jumper, then the next. The sticks poured out, each jumper leaning on the man in front of him so charged were they to get out the door. It was an adrenaline rush like no other. Even watching it made my heart pound.

Then the impossible happened again.

"Shit!" Jerry yelled over the intercom.

I sensed it even before we knew what he was talking about. Something about the sound was wrong. One of the soldiers, a huge guy, four or five from the back on the left side tripped as he ducked to go out the door. Everyone else followed just the same. It took a moment for my brain to process what I saw but subconsciously I knew. I unbuckled my belt and was down in the cabin by the time Jerry made the call.

"Hung jumper!" he yelled, flipping his intercom to hot mike. "Left side! Climb, climb, climb!"

As I grabbed a harness from the wall Kevin chopped the power on the #1 engine. The angle of the cabin tilted up as I ran to join Jerry and see what we could do.

"Tailpipe Whisky, we have a hung jumper," Bud called on UHF. *"I say again, 1-4 has a hung jumper."*

That set the radios on fire with everyone wanting more information. I hit the peanut switches passing the radio panel, shutting off their garble to my headset.

This jumper wasn't inverted. He dangled with his head closest to the door and his feet down, whipping in the slipstream like a flag in a tornado. His head was down, the wind pushing his chin to his chest. It was clear he was out cold. Something had hit him in the head, probably another jumper. The fiberglass helmet he wore had come loose. While I watched, the slipstream caught it and yanked it clear. It sailed high to bounce against the horizontal stabilizer then disappear behind us. The soldier twisted in the wind, oblivious.

The loose static lines of the other jumpers flapped around him. His own line looped around his neck but loosely, caught on the butt of his rifle which was strapped across his chest. Had the rifle not been there or were the line to slip, I had no idea if it would strangle him or simply come loose and pull the parachute free instead.

"He's out," Jerry called. "I'm bringing him in!"

He reached across me for the Emergency Reel and flipped the switch to retract. The sleeve at the far end of the cable began moving forward in the cabin, gathering all the lines together and pulling them in. The jumper, eight feet from the door, started moving up.

I saw the problem first. Watching the action at an angle, a movement at the bottom of the door caught my eye. Most of the lines were loose and therefore dangled high as they dragged across the side of the fuselage. The line with the jumper, however, was weighted down and slid across the bottom corner where the airdrop platform mounted. The platform hadn't fit and our crew chiefs had cut the metal base to mold the form. They had done a good job but the edges at the corner were still ragged. Those edges now sliced through the jumper's line. Strands of cotton fiber popped loose from the line one after another and danced in the slipstream.

"Stop!" I yelled above the engines. Reaching across I slapped Jerry hard in the arm. He released the switch and looked down where I pointed. For the first time his face took on an expression other than apathy. This time it was horror.

"Oh, shit!" He pulled the cigarette from his lips and flicked it out the door. "Shit, shit, shit!"

"What is it?" Kevin demanded from up front.

Jerry pushed me out of the way – there was room for only one person in the door – and knelt down to see what he could do with the line.

"What is it?" Kevin said again.

"Pilot, we've got a problem," I said. "His line's cutting on the door. If we try to pull him in it'll break through."

"What? Use the reel."

"We were using the reel! It's the static line itself. It's chafing on the platform – "

At that I had a thought and shouted it to Jerry. Kevin was thinking the same thing.

"So pull the platform out. Get it out of the way."

But Jerry said no, grabbing my hand and pointing. The platform swung inward once the cotter pin was released. There were already shards of metal sticking through the soldier's line – if the ledge swung more they would have to come with it, putting more pressure on the material that remained. The only way to keep them free was to pull the ledge straight back toward the front of the cabin. Unfortunately there was an entire fuselage in the way.

"We need to raise the line!" Jerry yelled. "Pull with me!"

He snaplinked his restraint harness to a tie-down ring on the floor between the troop doors. From there it gave him just enough movement that he could reach to each door without falling out. Now he extended the harness and leaned out the opening. The wind caught his right hand and blew it back but he fought to bring it down to the soldier's line. I grabbed him around the waist and tightened my own harness which I'd hooked further up in the cabin.

"What's going on?" Kevin said, frustrated that he couldn't see. He was flying now and holding us in a shallow, climbing spiral above the town of Sava.

"I...can't...see..." I grunted, holding onto Jerry and trying to dig my feet in.

Jerry reached for the soldier's line on the far side of the cut. He got one hand on it, then the other, but it was a thin cotton strap. An inch and a half wide and nothing thick, there was little to hold onto unless he could loop it around his wrist. The slipstream prevented that by keeping the line taught. Jerry pulled but got nothing. He reached out further but the line slipped through his hand. When his grip slipped he fell backwards and scraped his right arm across the platform. The metal slivers there opened up a cut that streamed blood, drops flying up and out the door.

"Goddammit!" he yelled, giving up.

"Mike, dammit, I need to know what's going on!" Kevin yelled angrily.

I helped Jerry out of the door. "The soldier's hung up six feet from the door, the static line is caught on the jump platform and we can't move it out of the way without slicing through the line. If we try to reel him in the same thing will happen."

"Can you reach him?"

"No! If we could reach him he would be inside by now! And Jerry just sliced up his hand trying."

Kevin motioned to Bud. "Go help them."

Bud scrambled out of the co-pilot's seat.

"He's too far out!"

"Mike, stay calm. I can't see so you tell me what my options are. You're telling me I've got a hung jumper that you can't bring in. Can you cut him loose?"

"He's unconscious!"

"Then you have to bring him in, Mike! Figure out something and do it quick. We were at bingo for the drop. We're now 400 pounds below. I can keep us airborne another 15 minutes but more than that we're going to be dead-sticking it in."

Well, hell, what did he want me to do? While Jerry wrapped his hand I knelt down in the door myself. The ground outside was getting farther away. I guessed we were at about 4,000 feet now.

Outside there was nothing to hold onto, nothing to grab except the static line itself. With my left hand on the door jam I tried that and did no better than Jerry. The line slipped through my fingers. Even when I got a grip I couldn't hold it tight enough to pull in 250 pounds of GI Joe.

"Can we land with him out here?" I asked desperately.

"We'll kill him," Kevin said.

"Can you slow down?"

"We're hanging on a stall now, dude."

"What if we lower the nose..." I was grasping at straws.

"This isn't the movies. You can't get him in?"

I looked at the man caught in the slipstream. Every few seconds, even in a left turn the slipstream spun him sideways and threw him against the fuselage.

"I don't know how."

Kevin paused a long time.

"You'll have to cut him," he said finally.

"How many times do I have to say it? He's unconscious."

"Has he got an automatic opener?"

"On a static line? From 1,000 feet? What do you think?"

Bud appeared next to me. He came back without a parachute or a harness but before I could say anything Jerry pushed between us to try again. Of all of us Jerry was the most frustrated. Jumpers were his responsibility. For all his crusty 19-year-master-sergeant-who-didn't-give-a-damn attitude, on this he gave a damn.

"We have to move the platform," he growled and pointed to the line. "This is not going to last."

We looked over his shoulder. Jerry was right. The line was giving way where it had snagged on the ledge. The steel slivers that came through it were opening wider holes with each spin of the jumper outside. A tear had opened at the edge of the material. Perhaps 60% of the line was still intact. There was no telling at what point it would fail catastrophically.

"Don't bank so much!" I called. "It's cutting the inside of the line. Come right 5 degrees."

"Right five," Kevin answered.

"Altitude?" Bud inquired.

"6,000 feet," Kevin replied.

The blood from Jerry's hand seeped through the dirty rag he tied around it. It mixed with the oil stains to form rusty blotches that blended with his flushed skin. He positioned us behind him.

"I'll lift," he motioned to me. "You pull the key and swing that damned thing out of the way. Once it's gone I can loop the line and pull him in. L-T, you keep me from falling out."

It would have looked funny under other circumstances. There was room for only one person in the doorway yet here were three of us trying to get our hands on the same thing. Jerry stood instead of kneeling this time, his legs wide apart as he bent to get one hand around the static line and pull it as straight up as he could. Big Bud grabbed Jerry around the waist as an anchor the way I'd done earlier. I crawled beneath the two of them to get at the cotter key on the aft side of the ledge.

"Ready?" Jerry called, the wind roaring in his mike again.

"Ready."

Minutes went by. It was taking too long. Even with the left engine dead and Kevin in a turn a hundred miles per hour of wind beat up the soldier and tugged furiously on the line.

Frantic suggestions fought in my head. Could the chute open on its own? What if we just pulled on the line ourselves and tried to loose it from the rifle? Pull on it ourselves? Great idea, moron. You can't even get a grip on it so how the hell will you get it off the gun?

I pushed on the ledge to get pressure off the pin.

"Ready!"

"Altitude?" Bud asked again.

"Eighty-two," was Kevin's automatic answer. He had the nose high enough that we could feel the rumble of an impending stall over the wing roots. Our one engine on full power clawed us skyward as fast as it could. Below, sunlight finally streamed across the valley floor. It made the air sparkle and threw splashes of orange across the door.

"Fuck the altitude," Jerry barked. "Pull."

He got his hand under the line on the far side of the cut and lifted straight up. At first nothing happened. Then the shards of metal that gripped the line gave way. Some cut more of it as they passed but for the moment the line held. I yanked the cotter pin out. The ledge came in on its own, the air pressure shoving it so hard it slammed against my shoulder with enough force to make fireworks go off in my head. I swung it aside and got to my feet.

"Now!" Jerry yelled. He spun away from Bud and wrapped his arm around the static line, finally free to get a good grip on it. I took Bud's place, grabbing his waist to help.

"PULL!"

We pulled. We weren't Tony Clovella and none of us had worked out with Major Harmon, but now adrenalin made us more than a match for either of them. The line moved. The slice in the line retreated from where it had been caught in the corner and the soldier moved two feet closer to the door. Big Bud grabbed the door jam and leaned down to seize the man's collar the instant he came within range. It was working. The soldier was on his way in.

And then the line broke.

Cotton was cotton and it had done all it could. As Jerry and I heaved the static line separated cleanly.

We fell back as though thrown, sailing into the middle of the cabin where Jerry landed on top of me. The soldier disappeared and the remaining line went with him, whipping out the door so fast Big Bud had no time to reach for it.

I tried to get a word out but nothing came. I'd never felt such a sense of horror in my life, not even at Calzada Larga. Bud was in the door looking outside and down. If there was anyone in the world who felt worse than me just then it had to be him.

"AAUUURRRRGGGHHHH!" Jerry yelled. He rolled off me and got to his hands and knees. With his bloody hand he pounded the floor.

"Load?" said Kevin. "Mike?"

"He's gone," I gasped, straining to breathe.

"What?"

The radios crackled. It was Walt again.

Nothing would fix this, I knew. The jumper at Calzada Larga had haunted me for weeks. In nightmares I saw him falling through 300 feet, face up, arms and legs flailing, straps from his parachute whipping around him but doing nothing to slow him down. Then he smacked the ground so hard that he bounced high above the sawgrass and broke into pieces. There were times when I couldn't close my eyes without seeing him. This would be worse.

Jerry stayed on his knees. His bloody hand was a mess. Scrunched in the center of the cabin, he held his head and didn't speak.

"Mike?" Kevin pleaded.

"He's...gone, Kevin," I forced myself to say. "The line broke."

Kevin stayed cool. "Mark," I heard him say and knew he was pressing the button on the INS to fix our position. It would help in finding the body.

"We've got to land," he said next. "We're on fumes. One of you get back up here."

Not me. I was in no condition to fly.

"Bud, it's all you," I mumbled into the mike.

There was no answer.

"Bud?"

I lifted my head but Bud was no longer in the door. I twisted to look up front, thinking he was already on his way to the cockpit. Nothing.

I vaulted to my feet.

"Pilot, is Bud up there?"

"What?"

"FUCK!"

Jerry looked up, then at the door. He spun on his knees and threw himself headlong at the sill.

Walt confirmed everything for us.

"Hey, Shark 14, I count two in the air. How many alibis did you have?"

I jumped into the copilot's seat.

Kevin banked left and chopped the throttles. We dove for the surface but it was a futile effort to see anything so small as a person against the ground. Even parachutes were hard to make out floating above the green surface. A body? Forget it. He never offered me the controls which was just as well.

"Oh, man," was the only thing he said. "Ohhhh, man..."

Trujillo was twenty-five miles away. At 3,000 feet we leveled out and pointed that way. By this time the fuel gauges were so low the needles barely registered. The Fuel Low lights had been on for a while.

"How did he fall out?" Jerry demanded. "How did he fall out?!"

Kevin looked at me.

"He...he wasn't wearing a harness," I remembered.

Walt had stayed with us throughout the ordeal, orbiting wide at 5,000 feet. When our soldier fell he had tried to keep him in sight. Now he was off our left wing a thousand yards. He had to be out of gas, too.

"Shark 13, Shark 13, this is Tailpipe Whisky."

It was the unsure voice of the Riverine.

"Tailpipe Whisky, go," Walt replied.

"Uhhhh, we have....eh, one parachute..." The squelch broke, static erupting into our headsets. Then we heard *"...in the river. Eh, we are moving to pick up. That was not so nice."*

Everyone in our cockpit had the same look on his face. What the hell was that? Two guys just packed it in and that's all they could say? It was *"not so nice?"*

For once, Walt declined to answer.

Our two planes flew the rest of the way to Trujillo in silence. We had long-since punched the Satcom and HF radios off and nobody thought to turn them on now. Kevin, perhaps, was wondering what he would report, how things could have gone from smooth to fucked-up so fast. I tried to come to grips with Bud getting sucked out the door and knew the nightmares were just piling up. Jerry stayed in the cabin. He never even bothered to close the troop door. The smell of cigarette smoke told us he was planted on the fold-down seat and dealing with demons of his own.

It was only after we landed that we found out what happened, that the Riverines had watched the whole thing and already called it in to Warlock.

Carl Diehrmann practically danced his way out of the bohio. Normally staid and cynical, he leaped about punching the air with both fists. He, too, had attended the Academy.

"Caught him at *two-thousand-fucking* feet!" he exulted, doing twirls on the ramp as we climbed down the steps. Our number two engine was still spinning down but the number one had quit on its own.

"What?"

"That stupid-looking, homeless homo Boo Radley copilot of yours caught him!" he repeated.

"At two thousand feet. It took him a thousand to get the chute to open and another five hundred to slow down. The locals thought they were going to pack it in. But no way, man! Not a Zoomie! HE FUCKING CAUGHT HIM!! They landed in the river, just outside the LZ. The Hondurans picked them up. No word on the Ranger yet but Bud's in one piece."

"He's alive?" I stuttered. Then, "He jumped?"

"He didn't fall?" Jerry demanded.

Carl grinned maniacally. "Jumped!" he affirmed. "Without a fucking chute! How does he get his balls in his pants??!! Give that man the biggest medal we've got but don't ever let me fly with him because he is out of this world crazy. Crazy like a loon. C-R-Z-Y, crazy!"

With a whoop and holler Carl led us to the bohio to listen to the radio ourselves. It was a confusion of chatter but one thing was clear. Bud had reached a thousand.

I wondered if it counted if you went without a chute.

2. Ecuador

IN MID-MARCH OF 1991 a farmer named Pedrado Momen searched for firewood in the Condor Mountains on the back side of Ecuador's Andes. Like all peasants in the area he spent hours each week foraging for wood. It was the only source of ready fuel to cook, boil water, and ward off the chill of the high thin air in the cordillera that rose between the Zamora and Santiago rivers. Coal or fuel oil would have been more efficient but there was none to be had in the region. Such things had to come from the coast. But they couldn't come from the coast. Logistics and human nature prevented it.

Logistically, it was all but impossible to bring anything in quantity to the Chinchipe region. There were no roads and only two navigable rivers. The terrain was steep, the forests thick, and in the rainy season valleys became seas of mud as water washed down the mountains. Even if transport wasn't an issue the laws of the market were. No commercial supplier of fuel oil would send it to the Condor mountains. The few people who lived there had no way to pay for it. That left the government to fill the energy gap. Theoretically, Lima could dictate a pipeline be built but it had no reason to do so. Fujimori and the Congress were short on money and also had other priorities. Hyperinflation, corruption, and car bombs going off in the cities took precedence over building infrastructure in an area of the country as populated as western Kansas. Chinchipe had no clout.

So Momen picked up wood. Striding stiffly along the spine of a ridge, a load of dry pine balanced on his shoulders, his calloused feet picked out flat areas on the uneven path.

At some point, by chance he noticed and picked up a small rock the size and texture of a granada fruit. It was malleable and had a yellow stripe and seemed to have rolled free from a fissure off the path. Momen liked the color of the rock so he tucked it in his shirt. In doing so he started a war.

I was glad he did. For when I returned from Quito in January after three weeks of studying Spanish the only souvenir I had was a map of Ecuador. So conflict in the country offered a chance to return and see it again.

The map came from the *Instituto Geográfico Militar*, the Ecuadorian army's Geography School. The school was one of those places I never intended to visit but Karla, the teen-aged daughter in the family I lived with while studying, pointed it out one day while we were out for a walk.

The school had a gift shop. The gift shop had maps. Geographical, topographical, hydrographical – any kind of map you wanted. All were of Ecuador, however, with just a few showing South America as a whole. When I asked for a map of Peru – knowing that Peru and Ecuador were always at odds – the young sergeant behind the counter advised me such information was not available "for security reasons." I thought it would have been just the opposite – that maps of Ecuador weren't available for "security reasons," since Peru, the enemy, presumably had maps of its own country – but didn't argue.

Every map was precisely and professionally drawn. Mountain ranges, rivers, coastline, and jungle were painstakingly detailed with color coding and contour lines to chart the elevation and foliage. Except...something was different. Every one of the maps had an anomaly which became obvious only when I looked at the few copies that showed the entire continent: Ecuador seemed bigger than I had remembered.

In fact, it *was* bigger. The mapmakers had changed the border. Or rather, they had not changed the border but had left in place the one that existed prior to 1942, the date of the last major war between Ecuador and Peru. At that time, while the rest of the world was occupied with defeating Germany and Japan, Peru had taken advantage of the turmoil to carve a swath of Amazon from its northern neighbor and keep it for itself. The chunk taken was the size of America's southwest, including Texas, and represented a good third of Ecuador's territory. Ecuador protested and looked north for redress but the U.S. played down the squabble in its backyard. For reasons of international politics the Roosevelt administration let the land-grab stand. It could hardly let itself be distracted by a Third World tiff when the future of democracy was at stake. The U.S. therefore sought to get the combatants and their neighbors to resolve the border issue. It brokered a settlement called the Rio de Janeiro Protocol which, in recognizing the theft, legitimized it. Brazil, Venezuela, Colombia, and everyone else in the region signed on. As a result, every map of South America that I had ever seen had a constant, familiar shape to all its countries that included an arching northeastern hook to Peru. The hook was the stolen territory and it hung poised over the current Ecuador like the upper jaw of a hungry anaconda.

And Ecuador felt its presence. It neither recognized nor accepted the loss of its jungle territory, what it called *el Oriente*, the East. Its maps reflected that stance.

"*Sí*," said Karla, tracing her elegant fingers over the red line that cut across her country. " *'La Zona en la que el Protocolo de Río de Janeiro es inejecutable,'*" she read. "*Y aquí está la linea que va a la otra frontera. No es legal. Esa parte es nuestro país, nuestro territorio. Es el Oriente. No importa lo que dice el Perú.*"

So there. She and her classmates were taught that regardless of what Lima's government might claim, the eastern territories belonged to Ecuador and one day they would get them back. I liked the attitude. I liked Karla. They were both unrealistic but principled. So I bought the map.

The southern portion of the Protocol line ran through the Cordillera del Condor, the Condor Mountains. However, there was a break in the line. Apparently in the 1940s even the Peruvians couldn't decide exactly where they needed the border to be. The mountains in the Condor region were so rugged that nobody was sure how to delineate a border. The compromise everyone reached in Rio de Janeiro was that the border would split "halfway between the watershed of the rivers Zamora and Santiago." Unfortunately for the lawyers, later surveys revealed that those two rivers did not share the same watershed – there was actually a third river basin, the Cenepa, that ran between them. In the 1960s Ecuador seized on that technicality to affirm the larger legal point that the whole treaty made no sense. Peru ignored the complaint, having on its side the reality of troops on the ground. And the outside world paid no attention.

That was how things stood for fifty years. Occasionally there were border clashes and once in the 1970s skirmishes continued for months with infantry battalions wandering through the jungle and floating down rivers to shoot at each other, but neither country was strong enough, rich enough, or interested enough to push the issue for long. Then Pedrado Momen discovered gold.

To anyone who knew anything about the Chinchipe region the "discovery" of gold was no surprise. Geologists from Ecuador and Peru as well as outside countries had known for a long time that the Condor region was rich in minerals: gold, of course, but also copper, tungsten, and tin. But the timing of Momen's find was fortuitous. In Peru, Alberto Fujimori had just come into office. While his preeminent concern was stamping out the Shining Path guerrillas, nationalism and support for the Peruvian military were closely related pillars of his administration. Forcing an issue with Peru's longtime rival Ecuador dovetailed neatly with his other shows of strength.

In Ecuador, on the other hand, economics more than anything else shoved nationalism into the public light. With the *sucre* perennially weak and unemployment running over 25%, the administration of Rodrigo Borja eagerly seized the gauntlet tossed before it. The opposition was knocking at the gates of power and had already taken over control of Congress from his Democratic Left party. A patriotic issue manipulated the right way could distract the public and solve financing problems at the same time.

So in late April of that year there was another war, the Cenepa War, focused on a 120-mile line that ran northeast roughly from the southern Lagunillas range to the headwaters of the Santiago river.

The terrain there was what flyers called the "low Andes": wet, jagged foothills of the main range. Peaks there reached over 10,000 feet. Valleys between the peaks dropped almost to sea level and lay carpeted in either sub-alpine coniferous forest or jungle.

The foliage wasn't the only thing that varied. The extremes of elevation over short distances meant extremes of climate as well. Bare mountain crags loomed over dusky jungle. Snow clung to high-altitude bowls while thousands of feet below parrots and macaws raced through the trees. In the valleys visibility could be perfect on a sunny day or nil when rains from the east ran up against the Andean wall. Rivers ran clear and cold. They cut through precipitous ravines while forest and fog hid waterfalls that humbled cataracts of the Colorado Rockies. In places rivers were the only clear areas that allowed an airborne observer to see to the ground. Curving, predictable courses, they promised to take you exactly where the map predicted – when they were on the map at all. It was rough terrain, frustratingly rough, but perfect for a tough little plane.

"So tell me again why we're doin' this?" Mick Connor said into his microphone as we bounced around at 18,000 feet.

We were feeling our way through clouds above the pass at Cuenca and having a rough time of it. Mick's red face looked pained and uncomfortable in the turbulence. I could tell from the thickness of his Boston accent that he didn't like being in the weather. Whenever Mick was worried his Beantown twang grew more pronounced. When he reached the stage of talking like a fishmonger at Faneuil Hall the rest of us could understand only half of what he was saying.

"I mean, here we are, flyin' through a frickin' thunderstorm tryin' to get to the frickin' Land That Time Forgot, and for what? So these two frickin' banana republics can keep throwin' rocks at each other across a piece of ground even my sister's smart enough not to want? What the frick is up with that?"

When Mick was stressed he was also useless as a co-pilot. He went through the training program just after Rolo and I did and – like us – got knocked around a fair amount by Captain Fetterman. Now, like Rolo, he was determined that in the seconds before any crash he would be sure to get a few choice words about his favorite instructor onto the cockpit voice recorder. It was disconcerting to me to know that in tight situations half our squadron could be counted on to start composing epitaphs.

"What does your sister have to do with this?" I said, trying to hold the plane level. Our altitude jumped around from 17,600 to 18,500 and there wasn't much I could do about it. I wasn't worried, though. At this location we were a good three thousand feet above the highest terrain so we weren't going to hit the ground. As for other traffic, we weren't on a published air route so it was unlikely we would run into another plane even if one happened to be out there. The big sky-little plane theory applied at times like this.

"Hey, leave my sister out of this!"

"I don't even know your sister."

"Then why'd you bring her up?"

"I didn't, you... never mind. Do you want to fly? You're getting all worked up over there. Maybe it'll take your mind off things."

"Like dyin'? Naww, you keep it. If I fly all I'll think about is smackin' the side of a mountain or havin' our wings ripped off in the middle of this frickin' thunderstaawwm. You keep it, yoaw the expewht."

"I'm the what? The expert? Why am I the expert? I've been here three months longer than you. And this isn't a thunderstorm. It's just a bunch of cumulus buildups that should quit as soon as we get past the mountains."

"It's a thunderstaawwm," he insisted, picking up the approach plate that came flying out of the holder by his knee. "And why do we have to be flyin' to this side of the mountains? Why can't we take their food someplace by the coast?"

"Because they're not *by* the coast. They're in the jungle."

"Well, let's tell them to move."

"What? Mick, when you were a child were you kidnapped and beaten by Andean peasants?"

"No."

"Then what do you have against the mountains?"

"I don't have anything against the mountains. I have something against *smackin'* the mountains.

I have something against being in the weather *over* the mountains."

"Why?"

"'Cuz that's when you run into things. When you're flying over the mountains and you can't see them."

"We're at 18,000 feet," I reminded him.

"We're at 17,700," he corrected me, pointing at the altimeter.

"Okay, we're at 17,700. Big deal, we're bouncing around. The highest peak around here is... is..." I fumbled with the map that he threw up on the dash. Mick grabbed it away again and jabbed his finger triumphantly at a spot.

"18,200!" he announced.

"But that's forty miles south of here!"

"Doesn't matter. How do you know we are where you think we are?"

"Because the navaids say we are! AND because I have a co-pilot who's supposed to be carefully monitoring our position."

"Well, I *am* monitoring our position and I recommend we teuhn back west."

"Why would we go west?"

"Why should we go east?"

I shook my head. How could we be having this conversation?

"Mick, we're going to the east side because that's where the fighting is. That's where the observers are. That's where the whole reason we're in Ecuador is. Hello? Have you not been paying attention the last three weeks?"

And then I remembered that Mick had a reason to hate the mountains.

Just after Christmas he and I had been part of a two-ship formation airdropping Colombian troops into a town north of Medellín. We had picked up the troops in Barranquilla, on the north coast, under the pretext of taking them to Bogotá and had filed our VFR flight plans accordingly. So after the drop we were obligated to continue to Bogotá even though we had no reason to go there.

The skies at Medellín were clear but the weather around Bogotá was, as a British commercial pilot reported over the radio, "dodgy." There were thunderstorms everywhere and they were embedded, meaning they were hidden in other clouds. The radar showed blips of red all over the sky. New blips popped up like flak over wartime Germany, forcing us to re-plot our course as often as we looked at the radar. Our formation split up and took spacing of thirty miles.

Declan and Mick were in the lead aircraft. I was flying with Jem. Fifty miles out the weather closed in and rain beat on the windscreen. For a while Declan radioed back regular reports of what the weather was doing and how bad the turbulence was up ahead. Then there was silence. It continued long enough for me to get uncomfortable. Finally I called them.

"*Uh, hey, Shark 18. You guys still up there?*"

Silence. I waited a few minutes.

"*Shark 18, this is Shark 19.*"

Nothing.

Jem and I looked at each other. We were still at 15,000 feet but Declan and Mick would have descended by now in anticipation of their approach. The highest terrain on our flight path was at 12,700 but the mountains on either side were higher.

"Maybe they can't hear us," Jem drawled.

"They've been hearing us all day," I answered. What could be wrong?

"*Shark 18, Shark 19.*"

Water dripped from the track on my side window. It landed on the intercom panel and splashed my leg.

"*Shark 18, Shark 19.*"

Suddenly, a reply: "*Shark 19, standby.*"

The call came quickly, curtly, barely getting out before Declan released the button. He didn't sound happy.

We stood by, not calling him back.

At fifteen miles the rain reached its peak. Lightning flashed all around. The plane jumped and bucked as it rode the currents sent up and down by the changing conditions. The only reason we continued was that the airport controllers at Bogotá itself said they had good weather. They lied. It was hard keeping the C-27 level much less on altitude and on course. When we entered holding northwest of the city it felt as though the wings would shake themselves right off the fuselage.

Jem flew a rough, scary ILS approach down to 800 feet where we finally broke out and got the runway in sight. Good weather, I suppose, is relative. To a guy sitting in an office looking out the window thunderstorms are probably cool. But we never heard another word out of Shark 18. I didn't relax until we pulled into parking and saw Declan's plane already in the chocks.

When we pulled up their loadmaster, Jerry Miner, was sitting on the ramp smoking two cigarettes, one in each hand. Declan was collapsed on the crew steps while Mick paced back and forth in the rain, swearing up a storm to rival the one blowing overhead.

What had happened was this: Just as they entered the published holding pattern twelve miles from the airport, at 12,000 feet and with the highest terrain over their heads and spitting distance away, a bolt of lightning that could have powered Europe arced across the sky and sent their navigational compasses spinning like roulette wheels. Static fouled their radios. In a turn, in the weather, turbulence throwing them around – for several seconds they couldn't talk to anybody and had no reliable way of telling if they were still in the protected area of the holding pattern. Then things got bad.

The GPWS, the Ground Proximity Warning System, which is a recorded voice that tells you when you're getting close to the ground, suddenly started barking at them. They weren't anywhere near the ground – the holding pattern was over the valley – but rain poured over the nose so heavy it prompted radar signals in the cone to think the ground was getting close. And since the compasses were spinning Declan and Mick couldn't be sure. The red *Pull Up!* light on the panel in front of each pilot suddenly flashed and the frantic, robotic tones of the audio warning screamed into the intercom: "PULL UP! PULL UP! TOO LOW! TOO LOW!"

Declan nearly had a heart attack. Mick probably did, keying the intercom and screaming, "Fetterman's a nazi! Fetterman's a nazi!" until Declan told him to shut up. Thinking they were about to hit the side of a mountain he reacted by shoving the power levers full forward and pulling the nose of the aircraft up as far as he could without stalling. Before the warning system ceased barking at them they shot through the holding patterns of two commercial jetliners above them, avoiding a mid-air collision by who knows how much. The big sky-little plane theory in action once again.

They had been lucky and they knew it. From the looks of it on the apron both men were still getting their coronary systems under control.

So now, over Ecuador, I decided to give Mick a break. An experience like that would stick with a guy.

But we still weren't turning back to the west. The war wasn't over. There was an armistice in place but no peace and for now a bunch of neutral countries had to monitor the ceasefire. One place they did that was outside a village called Patuca deep in the Cenepa region. A contingent of international observers sat there on a hillside making sure Peru and Ecuador didn't attack each other again. It was boring, uncomfortable duty, killing time in a harsh landscape while waiting for something to happen. For a change, today they were waiting for us and I didn't want to disappoint them.

I didn't want to disappoint them partly because that was our job – when we told somebody we would land someplace at an appointed time we needed to do it. It made for a good reputation besides being the professional thing to do. Professionalism aside, however, I wanted to land at Patuca today because we were carrying food.

Lots of food. Clunk, our loadmaster, was sitting on one pallet of dried goods and two filled with fresh vegetables, fresh eggs, and frozen meat. The back of the plane looked like a Safeway loading dock, packed high with three mounds covered by plastic tarps and cargo netting. Each pallet was so wide that our fourteen passengers were spread out in seats on both sides of the cabin with little room to put their feet. They propped them on boxes of oranges, apples, pears, and grapefruit that lined the edges of the pallets. Crates of lettuce and broccoli clustered at the forward end. Gallons of tomatoes were packed into tins in the center. Cartons of mushrooms, jars of onions, baskets of garlic and zucchini – all made an appearance. There were carrots. There was a cardboard tub of watermelon. There were cantaloupe and mangos and white melons and sweet corn and celery. There was even a container of turnips. We were flying a salad bar over the Andes.

But what the guys on the ground really wanted to see was the meat. The last pallet – the one closest to the ramp where the plane never got warm – had all the frozen goods: 50 lbs of bacon, six turkeys, a dozen chickens, eight slabs of ribs that would have done any barbecue proud, and a side of beef that it took three men to lift onto the pallet. Three big men. Everyone commented the instant they saw it, "That's a big piece of beef," and they were right. I felt like a butcher's delivery man.

The irony was there were only forty-some people at the Patuca site. Foreigners, that is. There were three dozen American guardsmen from the States, a couple of regular Army troops from Fort Gulick in Panama, two Brazilian soldiers, one civilian each from Argentina and Chile, and an engineer from Venezuela. The Ecuadorians had their own camp on station – on the other side of the airstrip where we would land – but technically we weren't supplying them. This was a morale run, a shipment to lift the spirits of the people who had been uprooted from their normal jobs and dropped into Remotesville, South America with no warning. They were all sitting on the side of a hill in a tight canyon upstream from the muddy village of Patuca and there wasn't Thing One around in the way of entertainment, escape, or leisure.

There wasn't a whole lot of food, either. The recent fighting between Peru and Ecuador took everyone by surprise, including the participants. The logistics of fighting a war in such inhospitable terrain needed time to catch up with events, and fresh food was on no one's priority list.

Worse, the group at Patuca had no homeward flights on the calendar. Plunked on a remote hillside in suffocating jungle with nothing but tents, canned food, and water purification tablets, they hunkered down and waited to be forgotten, their vaguely-defined mission lost in the bureaucracy of humanitarian interventions.

"See? It's breaking up."

The clouds opened as we flew past Gualeceo. They closed again but only briefly. From there on we popped in and out of scattered pockets of light rain and mist. Mick was visibly relieved. By the time we cleared the Andes proper the ceiling lifted to twenty thousand feet and we had clear air all around.

Clear everywhere but down, that is.

"Oh, this doesn't look good," Clunk said, leaning over my shoulder.

We were in the clear at our altitude but below us a solid deck started at ten thousand feet, blocking out any view of the ground. We had no idea how far down it went.

"No," I agreed. "Anybody see any holes?"

Nobody did. The blanket of clouds stretched to the horizon. To the south we could see mountain peaks and behind us was the weather we had just flown through but there was nothing out front poking up from the jungle to give us a bearing.

I wasn't worried about getting lost. We knew where we were, mostly. Reading the map was out since we couldn't see the ground but our instruments still picked up the Cuenca VOR radio. Even the DME, the distance transmission associated with the VOR, came through intermittently. Best of all our INS had us dead-on and pointed our final leg toward the Namangoza Valley, near the bottom of which lay Patuca.

We descended to the top of the cloud deck to confirm its height. At 10,500 feet we brushed the first tendrils that whipped above the cloud like meringue. The deck itself was thick and consistent. We surfed it for miles riding the feathery swells, never dipping in so that we lost visibility and never varying our altitude more than five hundred feet. Then we climbed back up to fifteen thousand to view a wider area.

"Five miles," Mick observed.

We were on course to the narrow Namangoza and about to overfly it at an oblique angle. Had it been clear we could have seen the camp and the airstrip. Had it been clear we would already have started our descent.

Implicit in his tone was the question: What are you going to do, aircraft commander?

To be honest, I wasn't sure. This was one of those many situations that the instructors mentioned in training but never gave good answers for.

"How are we doing on gas?" I asked.

We needed an hour's worth – 2,000 lbs – to return to Guayaquil from Patuca. We needed another thousand pounds on top of that to divert to the airport at Machala in case we couldn't get into Guayaquil for some reason. That made 3,000 lbs. I always added another five hundred for the wife and kids I hoped to have someday, bringing our bingo to 3,500. Anything on top of that we could use to explore ways of getting into Patuca.

"Well, there's always a hole," I said.

"You've been flying with Walt," Mick accused.

We flew over the field, nothing but cloud down below.

"Shark aircraft! Shark aircraft! This is Snapper!"

A delirious voice erupted over the FM radio. Snapper was the Patuca command post. That meant it was whoever had time to operate the radio.

"Shark aircraft! Shark aircraft! This is Snapper!" the voice repeated, positively euphoric.

"Jeez," said Mick. "He didn't give me a chance to answer."

"Snapper, this is Shark 24. Go ahead."

"Roger, Shark 24. Hey, we can hear you overhead! You're cleared to land. Ha-ha, we've got nobody else coming in today. Just park at the north end and you'll have a whole team of guys waiting there to unload you. Ha-ha! You won't have to do a thing!"

"Ha-ha!" Clunk repeated from the back.

"Yesssss, hmmmm," I said into the intercom. Mick winced. Clunk climbed up to the third seat and turned it forward. He shook his head.

"Sounds like we're going to have to kick their puppy," he said.

I motioned to the radio.

"You want to tell him that?"

"Oh, no, the pleasure's all yours."

"Well, we can still look for a while yet," Mick offered.

"Yes," I said hopefully. "Let's head east. Something might open up over the jungle."

"Hey, Shark 24! You still there?" the upbeat voice inquired.

"Uh, yeah, Snapper. Shark 24 still here."

"Yes, sir, did you copy that? We'll do the unloading. Um, some guys here just wanted to confirm: you have a big package for us, right? A lot of food?"

I debated what to say and then settled with, *"That's affirmative. We've got your food."*

"Word is you brought us 200 hundred pounds of steer. That's a big piece of beef!"

There was a sound of cheering in the background.

"Uh, roger."

Clunk slid back in his seat and made a kicking motion. Mick waved at him to take the mike but he shook his head.

I sighed, picking my words carefully.

"Say, Snapper. Listen, about the landing. We've got a little weather up here. What's it looking like down on the ground?"

The silence that followed my transmission was painful. All ground-pounders believe that all flyers are the laziest sacks of human waste ever to walk the earth. They think aircrew will do whatever they can to avoid accomplishing whatever mission they're on. We don't want to take off or we don't want to land or we don't want to fly somewhere because of weather or maintenance or bad hotels or crew duty day limitations... Whether that was the thought going through Snapper's head or whether he just had a sudden panic at the thought of his airborne feast vanishing like a mirage, the next call lost its cheery edge.

"The weather? Um,...it, uh,...well, the uh,...just a minute. Let me look."

"Oh, yeah! The weather!" said Mike sarcastically. "Come on, how do you not notice the weather?"

There was a brief pause on the radio.

"Uh, it's good! Come on in!"

Uh-huh.

"Okay, uh, can you quantify 'good'? Can you give us an estimate of how high the clouds are above the ground? We've got a layer up here that starts at ten thousand feet and goes on down so we can't see the

ground. Can you give us your best guess where they start above you?"

Another pause. There was some jockeying of the mike switch down on the ground and we briefly heard muffled voices. It sounded like an argument.

"Uh,..." came the call back. *"They're pretty high."*

"Can he quantify 'pretty high'?" Mick retorted.

"Right, Snapper. What would you say they are in hundreds of feet?"

More muffled conversation.

"Well, we're guessing here, but Sgt Decker says maybe four or five hundred feet."

"Copy, four to five hundred feet. Thanks. We'll call you back shortly."

"Uh, okay. Yeah, just let us know. You're still going to land, right?" The last question was desperate.

"We'll call you back. Shark 24, out."

"Who's Sgt Decker?" Clunk asked.

"I don't know."

"Well, he said 'Sgt Decker' like that's supposed to mean something to us," Mick said.

"It's probably just the guy who's in the tent with him."

"You want to head east?"

I eyed the fuel gauges. "Yeah, we've got the gas. Let's head east and find a hole."

Immediately east of Patuca was the Cordillera de Cutucu, a 6,000-foot-high ridge that formed the eastern flank of the Namangoza Valley. However, if we went north up the valley and then turned east we could stay over lower terrain while we looked for an outlet to the jungle. North lay several villages as well as the towns of Sucua and Macas. Sucua had an NDB which almost never worked. Macas had one that was better. In fact, the Macas NDB defined part of a low-altitude route that ran parallel to the mountains through the low Andes and therefore was generally more reliable. I say 'generally' because an NDB is one of the least-precise navigation signals out there in the world today. It's no better than most commercial radio stations, which means if you use it to guide your plane you're trusting your life to a talk show. That doesn't mean NDBs don't work, it just means that given a choice most pilots wouldn't use them as their sole means of feeling their way through mountainous terrain.

But we had no intention of descending into the clouds today, NDB or no. I wanted to stay visual, in constant sight of clear sky above or hard ground below, and I thought we had a way to do that.

My hope was that we could stay high until well out over the jungle where the terrain was flat and there would be no danger of smacking a hill that we wouldn't see if we descended into the clouds. Once there we would find a hole, descend to get below the cloud deck, then fly west again until we came back to the mountains. There we would find the Palora River, follow it up to the Upano River, take that down to Macas, and then right into the Namangoza Valley. Like following streets in Chicago. Simple. I explained it to the crew, both of whom mentioned that they'd never been to Chicago.

It all depended on finding a hole in the clouds.
"See anything?"
"No."
"Clunk?"
"No."
"I don't either. Try further south."

There was no way to spot a hole in the clouds other than to see it outright. There weren't anomalies in a cloud deck that hinted at a hole, such as a sudden build-up on one side or another or a change in the color. Because the jungle out here didn't change – it was thick green forest as far as the eye could see – when a cloud deck formed over it the deck didn't change, either. Our only hope was that the weather pattern that produced the deck wasn't perfect. Thick stratus layers result from warm fronts, low pressure regions, and a constant supply of moist air. Any imperfections – a warm front that wasn't uniformly warm, a low that wasn't low enough, an air mass that was more moist here and not-so-moist over there, or even a random wind – could create a pocket where the clouds just didn't close up. Nobody on our plane was a meteorologist but we knew how the jungle worked. Sometimes we got lucky.

"Hey, there's one," Mick announced. He banked right to a narrow gash in the clouds two miles off his wing. The gash became a canyon with narrow sides that funneled down to a very small outlet at the bottom. Through the outlet was a patch of dark green.

"Eewww," he said thoughtfully, his index finger on the mike. "It don't look good."

I leaned over from my side as he circled the cut. It didn't look good at all. Even if we banked it up tightly – and the C-27 could turn on a dime – this hole was small. Not more than a mile across at the top. Less at the bottom. We would be spiraling down an ever-shrinking drain. If at any point we needed to call it off and climb out there was no way we could do that and stay out of the clouds. It also wasn't clear from our vantage point – looking straight down – if the clouds stopped before they reached the trees. For all we knew the whole deck sat right on the canopy. That meant we could get to the bottom of the hole and be no better off than we were right now. In fact, we would be a lot worse.

"I don't think so," Mick concluded.

"I agree," I said.

"Make that three," Clunk tossed in. When Mick threw him a 'What do you know about it?' glance Clunk sniffed, "I couldn't drop a basketball into that hole so don't think you can *fly* down it."

We flew on.

Somewhere below us was the Palora River. It was the largest river in the area, wide and flat and perfect to fly over in a small plane as we sought to avoid trees and ground. But we couldn't see it.

There were other rivers on the map with colorful names. The Capahuari, the Ishpingo, the Huitoyacu. There were also settlements like Ipiak and Huasaga, Pumpuentsa and Surikentsa. All native names and all from far-flung languages and tribes.

How the words sounded wasn't as important as the fact that they were there at all. To see all the marked settlements on our map one would think there were people all over the ground below us yet the opposite was true. Presence on a map meant little out here. Symbols on paper didn't necessarily mean buildings on the ground. If these places existed at all it was unlikely they had more than fifty to a hundred inhabitants. Moreover, none of them had runways. Or roads. Or ports. This part of the jungle was only a few miles from the mountains and already it was remote.

It didn't take long for us to burn gas down to our bingo point. Bingo is the point at which you turn home and quit messing around, so that's what we did.

On our way back to the mountains we overflew Patuca again. I called Snapper to explain the situation. The radio operator was crestfallen.

"Oh,...well, Sgt Decker thinks the weather's getting better down here," he offered.

"There's that Sgt Decker again," Mick wondered. "Who *is* that guy?"

"Well," I responded as tactfully as I could, *"unfortunately we can't get there from here. We need to descend in clear weather to get down there and there isn't any of that up here."*

"Roger, we understand," he replied in a tone that suggested they clearly did not.

"But we'll be back in about three hours," I said. *"We'll go back to Guayaquil and refuel and try again."*

Snapper perked up immediately upon hearing that.

"Oh, okay! We'll be waiting!"

I expected Mick to grumble about making a second trip across the mountains but he didn't. Clunk didn't complain, either. He never did.

The passengers were all military, half a dozen Services and Finance people bringing mail, money, and paperwork for the troops below. A legal aide carried wills and powers of attorney for guys to fill out who had missed the chance before deploying. Funny that even out here in such a remote war zone bureaucracy could track you down.

One of the passengers was Major Leo Kradel, a staffer from the wing commander's office. He had boarded our plane at the last minute in Panama and said he was just going south to see how the Patuca operation was going. A day-trip to give the general an eyes-on. We worried about him at first, thinking he was grading us somehow, but so far all he had done was sleep.

We flew back to Guayaquil via the same route we took out: over Cuenca sitting in its picturesque bowl at the base of the Allcuquiro Ridge, then out over the steeply descending terrain of Azuay Province to the coast. The clouds there thinned and cleared, turning from a stratus layer to cumulus peaks that we dodged between. By the time the Pacific Ocean came into view we had sunshine above and clear air below. We could see the land everywhere as it sloped away from the Andes and down to the coast. There blue water dotted with shrimp farms led us north.

The airport at Guayaquil had an Ecuadorian military base in one corner. The base was a collection of little-cared-for buildings and mostly-empty parking ramps. The only plane in sight was an old DC-3 that looked as if no one had touched it in years. It sat in the grass twenty feet from the headquarters building, pointing its nose stubbornly above the horizon as though still willing to take off on a moment's notice.

On the military ramp was a small concrete building with one office and sometimes a soldier who could file flight plans for us and give us information on the weather. Sometimes. Most of the time the building was as empty as the overgrown lots around the ramp. Today there was a car parked outside the hut.

"Find a fuel truck, Clunk," I called over my shoulder as the props wound down, "and get us eight thousand pounds of gas."

Clunk opened the crew entry door and jumped out with the chocks.

"Sir," I said to Kradel, "Lieutenant Connor and I are going to file again and check the weather. As soon as we get our gas we'll be on our way again."

"No problem," he replied, yawning. "Take your time. This beats a day in the office. Is it alright if people stretch their legs?"

"Sure, by all means. If anybody wants to hit a bathroom they can follow us."

Of course everyone wanted to visit the bathroom so now a crowd of ten pushed through the door of the operations office. The soldier behind the counter looked up in alarm.

"That way," Mick pointed down a hallway at the back of the office. The legal aide, a young airman, handed her briefcase to one of the finance troops and hurried in that direction.

I smiled at the conscript and explained why we were back. I smiled again when he pulled the lone weather sheet off the clip on the wall and repeated exactly the same information he had given me four hours earlier. There was nothing to be updated here.

"Eight thousand," Clunk stated when Mick and I returned to the plane.

"Good. Nothing's changed on the weather. We'll just repeat what we did this morning – with more success, I hope. Everybody back?"

"Yeah. I get the impression they didn't like the bathroom."

"Really?"

The bathroom behind base operations was a small room with a hole where the window had been. It smelled but the toilet mostly flushed and the water in the sink was mostly clear. I wondered what the passengers would think of Patuca.

An hour later we were overhead Snapper again.

"*Shark 24, Snapper. I hate to say this, sir, but the weather's kind of gotten bad here.*"

That wasn't a surprise. The deck that had been at ten thousand feet was now at twelve thousand, and instead of being flat like a table it had geysers of thunderheads poking up sporadically to the horizon.

"*Really? What does Sgt Decker think?*"

In response to the looks I got from Mick and Clunk I replied, "I had to ask."

"*Uh, sir, Sgt Decker agrees it's gotten kind of bad.*"

"*Hmm, how high would you say the clouds are now?*" I asked.

"*Uh, well, sir, it's hard to say. We can't really see them through the rain.*"

Mick threw up his hands.

We held for an hour then returned to Guayaquil again. When we got there it was five-thirty. While Clunk took on more fuel I used the shortwave radio to call the Air Operations Center in Panama and ask if they wanted us to come home.

"*Negative,*" came the reply. "*You're to stay on station and deliver the cargo.*"

"*That'll mean staying the night here,*" I clarified to the radio operator. "*We won't be able to try again until tomorrow morning.*"

There was a pause before the reply came back. The operator was just some airman or sergeant manning the desk and undoubtedly he relayed my info to the officer on duty.

"*Understood.*"

I was afraid of that. Not that I ever minded a night off-station. But none of our passengers carried an overnight bag.

I found Major Kradel and explained the situation to him. He stroked his moustache, then shrugged.

"Well, that'll teach us to come prepared next time! I'll tell the others. You know, it'll be good for some of these troops. Most of them have never been down here, much less spent the night."

I breathed a sigh of relief. Some field-graders might have blown up over an unscheduled layover. I wouldn't have been happy myself to get stuck somewhere without so much as a toothbrush. As it was, Mick, Clunk, and I all had overnight bags with us – we never went anywhere without them. I knew the passengers would regard us with suspicion for it, suspecting that we had planned to spend the night all along.

"Aww, don't worry," Mick said. "The hotel will have those little shampoo packs for them to play with. They shouldn't complain."

"Easy for you to say," Clunk pointed out.

Our immediate problem, beyond getting a hotel, was the perishable nature of our cargo. In the heat of the equatorial coast even the frozen side of beef was starting to sweat by the time we landed for the third time. The Ecuadorian clerk who processed our flight plans listened to our dilemma. He came out to the aircraft to see it for himself.

"*Eso es mucho carne,*" he commented. "That's a big piece of beef."

He thought for a moment. When he came up with nothing he went back to his desk and called around to other offices on the field. Many of his conversations included an exasperated "*Sí! En serio!*" when whoever it was doubted his veracity. But when his index finger finally jabbed triumphantly into the air I knew he had found a solution.

"This isn't much of a solution," Mick said an hour later.

We stood in a walk-in freezer. The DC-3 was parked outside. I knew it was because I could see it through a hole in the freezer wall that was the size of my fist. While it was undeniably cooler in the room, it was cooler not like the Arctic but more like the basement of an old house. It was the best the locals had.

"*Gracias!*" I said cheerily to the clerk. With what I hoped was a sincere smile, I promised that this freezer would surely fix our problem.

And I thought it might. After all, we only needed one night of storage away from the outside heat. By tomorrow mid-morning, the side of beef and all its accessories would reach its intended consumers.

Twenty-four hours later I stood in the same spot.

"*Gracias*," I repeated stoically. The clerk looked doubtfully at the dripping mass of meat that three unshaven, unhappy Services troops carried in from the plane. A trail of watery red drops followed them.

"The weather was bad?" he asked, turning away as the beef, like a corpse from a grisly accident, was laid carefully on the freezer floor.

Mick glared at him in response. He'd spent the day bouncing around in thunderstorms.

"You might say that."

The weather had been bad. Even the troops at Patuca hadn't tried to hide it. They were getting rained on and winds through the valley exceeded thirty knots. At fifteen thousand feet we were in and out of clouds all day and didn't come close to finding a way to descend. Half our passengers became airsick.

The lettuce began to wilt.

Thursday morning the sky was overcast when we checked out of the hotel. By now everyone without luggage had picked up a toothbrush and razor and so looked presentable if weary. But no one had been able to do laundry. There were quite a few rumpled and rank members of our group.

The skies were rumpled over the Andes, too. Mick flew while I had another terse long-distance conversation with the AOC in Panama. Maybe it was the attenuation of my voice over the airwaves, maybe it was the historic lack of trust between us and the non-flyers in the vault who were always convinced that aircrews were scamming something, but the guys in Panama just didn't get what I was saying about our situation. Not having been in Ecuador, not having seen our walk-in freezer, they didn't appreciate that in another twelve hours the troops in Patuca would take our gift of fully-thawed turkeys and botulistic beef and dump it in the river, morale or no morale. The lieutenant colonel I spoke to insisted we get our cargo to its destination and all but implied I would be guilty of insubordination if we returned home without doing so. His order was simple: the food was not to return to Panama.

I signed off. Judging from the smell in the cabin, there was no danger of our cargo returning to Howard. I would dump it in the Pacific before riding with it another six hours. The fact that this time Clunk had packed the meat forward in the cabin and closer to the cockpit only made things worse.

"He didn't sound happy," Clunk observed.

"He sounded like it was national security or somethin'," Mick agreed. "What the hell is so frickin' important about carrots? Hey, Clunk. Check those turnips out. Are they really turnips or are we carrying parts for a *nucleah* bomb?"

"Well," I said, trying to stave off mutiny and convince myself at the same time. "Maybe we don't know the big picture. Maybe there's more to this trip than just food."

Major Kradel listened on a headset.

"No," he offered. "There's less. I'm not the most important guy in the wing but if there was a hidden agenda to this trip the general would have filled me in on it. He didn't so I think whoever that colonel was you were talking to is more concerned about his mission effectiveness percentages than he is about using his head. You're a flying supermarket, not the Enola Gay."

That fit. On my only other trip to Patuca I had carried an equally strange load: four Ecuadorian soldiers, two local folk singers, a pimp, and a prostitute. The woman had boarded the plane wearing a uniform but halfway through the flight stripped off the fatigues and replaced them with what looked like a burlap moo-moo fastened at the waist with rope. Imagine a Franciscan friar crossed with a Parisian hooker. It turned out the Ecuadorian contingent at Patuca had been there a lot longer than the international observers, long enough that they had an established rotation for USO-type entertainment. Call it Bob Hope-with-a-twist.

"How's it look?" Kradel asked. He had been so patient that we let him stay on headset and occasionally sit in the third seat. We kidded him only a bit about his odor.

"Like junk," Mick replied. "Sir."

He brought the map close to his face as we skipped in and out of clouds, determined to find the one mountain out there that was lurking for a kill. "We're going to have to airdrop this stuff after all."

"I don't know," Clunk replied. He leaned over Kradel's shoulder to look out the front windows. "It doesn't look as bad as yesterday."

I thought the same. There were just as many clouds and the layer was still at ten thousand but the colors weren't as menacing. Whereas on Tuesday and Wednesday slate-grey and thunderstorm-black had dominated, today the deck had more patches of white. There was a chance.

"How about if we try something different?" I suggested.

"Famous last words," Mick said.

"No, how about this: let's see if the Sucua NDB is up. If it is we can intercept a course to it and descend to 7,000 feet. After Sucua we can go as far as Macas on their signal if their beacon is up, too."

"You want to descend over an NDB?" Mick said in disbelief.

"No!" I replied at once.

I knew what he was suspicious about. Griswold Beckett, the senior idiot in our squadron, had tried to descend over a field TACAN up in Colombia. TACANs and NDBs work the same way when you're close to them – like junk. The needles just spin because the signal rises up like an inverse cone: if you're directly overhead the plane picks up nothing. Griswold tried to descend – in the weather, over the mountains – reasoning that as long as the needles were spinning he was over the navaid and therefore safe. The idea that just about anything else could make the needles spin, too – a malfunctioning transmitter, a broken receiver, bad weather – didn't occur to him because, as mentioned, he was an idiot. Kurt, his co-pilot, seized the controls and nearly beat Griswold to death with the crash axe. Griswold got beaten up by his copilots a lot.

"No!" I repeated. "I want to descend *using* the NDB."

"You want to descend in the weather on an Ecuadorian NDB?" Mick persisted.

"Sure, we do it all the time."

"No, we do it all the time in *good* weather, not thunderstorms."

"These aren't thunderstorms. Okay, okay," I backtracked as he protested, "they are thunderstorms. But we have the radar, the map, and the INS to back us up. I don't think there's any real risk so long as the signal's good and we stay over the valley."

Clunk was willing. He had a Low Rider magazine that got more interesting the worse it looked outside. He had been paging through it absentmindedly but now decided to start reading the articles. It kept his head down and his mind off what was outside the window. Still he threw us a thumb's-up.

Kradel gave his nod, too, though admitting that his navigator days were in the past and all he remembered about NDBs was that pilots hated to fly them. I swapped controls with Mick and took over map-reading duties.

We flew over Patuca and turned north by northwest.

Snapper got on the radio, depressed, unwilling to get his hopes up for our arrival after two days of disappointment. He said it was raining but not hard. Drizzle. He could see down the valley at least three miles. He knew it was three miles because there was a rope bridge that far that stretched across a ravine. Mick began a descent. We entered the clouds completely at 9,700 feet.

"I don't like this," Mick growled.

"Relax. The closest hill isn't until 6,000."

"So I have thirty-seven hundred feet to think about it."

We broke into the clear again at 8,500 feet. There we found a thousand feet of clear air until the next cloud deck began. That clear space was a startling, beautiful sight: above and below were endless layers of downy white and between them the clearest air imaginable.

"You want to go in there?" Mick asked as we descended, pointing to the lower deck. He was content to stay between layers.

"Sure," I said. "I'll bet it's thin, too."

It was, though not thin enough for my co-pilot's tastes. This layer went down to 5,500 feet before breaking up which meant that for five hundred feet Mick sweated worse than the beef in the cabin. We popped out in the clear between two rain showers, mountains visible on the right and left. A third deck below us spread over the lower hills like fog on a meadow but a shift in our groundspeed suggested that winds were beginning to play a part in the system. That boded well for a breakup.

And the clouds did break up. Here and there gaps in the third deck revealed the ground below, dark green slashes standing out in a white duvet of rolling cloud cover. The problem was they remained nothing but slashes. We flew over Sucua. The NDB wavered then spun in confusion, telling us we were over the navaid, but we couldn't see the town. I dialed the frequency for Macas. When the needle settled down pointing that way Mick checked it against our INS and tweaked our course to follow. He descended to 3,300 feet, the top of the third and lowest deck.

"You want to descend into this one?" he asked, his tone implying his own opinion.

I looked over my shoulder at Clunk who tore himself away from his magazine long enough to mouth, "no way."

"Nope," I said. "Let's find a good hole."

Some holes opened up but they weren't good ones. It wasn't enough to see straight down: we had to know that once we got down there we would be able to go somewhere.

We flew on to Macas – which we couldn't see, either – then over a low ridge to meet the Rio Pastaza just south of Palora. There the deck finally opened and we were able to descend and reverse course.

Rain showers came out of the deck on the bottom side and stretched down to the surface. Mick played a game of hunt-and-peck around them. Sometimes rain came out of nowhere and pattered against the windscreen hard enough to make the world outside a blur. But it always passed and the drops blew away. A straight line to Patuca was impossible but at 300 feet above the trees we could trace the map and the terrain.

"Wind's picking up," Kradel observed.

"That's gonna be bad for landing," Mick whined.

"You must be confident we'll to make it to the runway."

"Oh, we'll make it," he assured me. "You know why? Because it's scary inside that valley – scarier than it is out here. With my luck we'll make it."

He was right. At first it didn't look like we would get past Macas. A rain squall hovered over it. But Mick circled left and then crossed the river north of town. From that angle we could see the Patuca valley was clear.

"Ya know," Mick twanged, his nasal tone getting richer, "this meat is bad. If we die trying to land, I'm gonna have died for bad meat. Does anybody besides me see something wrong with that?"

"There's lettuce, too," Clunk shrugged, head buried in the pages. "Don't die for the meat, do it for the lettuce."

Past the squall we dropped back into the river basin to give ourselves clearance from both clouds and ground. It felt less claustrophobic that way. Ten miles to go.

"Twenty-two knots on the tail," I mused, looking at the ground speed indicator. I said it hoping that someone would contradict me. No one did and the takeoff and landing data chart on my leg said quite clearly that we wouldn't be able to stop with that much wind pushing us down the runway. But I didn't know what else to do. I hoped a solution would appear once we got to the field.

The problem with Patuca was that we could only land in one direction. There was jungle on the south side of the strip. The closest trees there stood up so high that we couldn't touch down soon enough from that direction to meet our roll-out requirements. The troops kept promising to cut them down but hadn't gotten to it yet. So if we were going to go in it had to be from the north.

"Gear down. Before landing checklist."

We talked it over. While we did Mike pulled left into a tight racetrack holding pattern just short of the narrowest part of the valley.

"Let me get this straight," Major Kradel said. "You don't have enough runway in one direction because of the wind, you don't have enough runway in the other direction because of the trees. Is that right?"

"That's it."

He looked over his shoulder at the mountain of rotting, wilting food and concluded, "You guys have the worst luck of anybody I've ever flown with."

Clunk finally gave up trying to ignore us and threw his magazine down.

"Oh, I don't know. We haven't hit anything yet. Hey, sir, how about a combat offload?"

I looked at him over my shoulder.

"At seventy miles per hour?"

A combat offload was usually done while taxiing. The loadmaster released the locks on the pallets and they rolled out the back and off the ramp.

"Why not? The book doesn't say we can't."

"The book's in Italian. We have notes from it in English."

"The notes don't say we can't."

"They don't say we can, either."

"So there. We're covered."

The good thing about flying a new airplane is that its manuals aren't all-inclusive. They can't be because the writers have no idea how a customer will actually try to use a machine. The bad thing about flying a new airplane is that by not covering everything the first group of pilots never has the luxury of benefiting from someone else's experience. As Lt Col Rasmussen would say, good judgment comes from experience and experience sometimes comes from bad judgment. The first group always has a lot of opportunities to exercise bad judgment.

"No," I decided.

Then I re-considered. We were light. Light enough that if we landed and couldn't stop by the end of the runway, we could always just take off again without slowing down. We could slow to 60 mph before we would have to initiate the go-around. Clunk could have the ramp open and waiting. The passengers could stay forward and out of the way. It was new; it was something we hadn't done before; it was one of those things that if it worked nobody would say a word and if we screwed it up would probably be banned forever. It was definitely bad judgment.

When I asked Mick he threw up his hands.

"One of my instructors always said it's better to ask for forgiveness than permission."

"Did he get in trouble a lot?"

"His *faehhh* share."

We circled one more time. I hated decisions like this. The safe course was to say no and give up. But I also hated pilots who always took the safe course.

"Clunk, what'll it do to our center-of-gravity?"

"Nothing, so long as none of the pallets snags a cargo strap on the way out and gets dragged behind us down the runway."

"Then let's do it. Run the Combat Offload Checklist."

Mick descended another hundred feet. We headed down the valley. Drops of rain pattered against the windscreen. We were now at two hundred feet. Being that close to the ground unnerved him almost as much as thunderstorms did so he hunched over the controls and fixed his eyes straight ahead.

"Snapper, this is Shark 24."

There was no reply. I repeated the call.

"Uh, Shark 24, go ahead."

Snapper's voice wasn't chipper anymore. The poor guy was becoming used to disappointment.

"Snapper, Shark 24. We're three minutes out. How does your weather look?"

When Snapper came back it was with a different voice, this one deep and gruff but trying hard to be deeper and gruffer than it was.

"Shark 24, this is Lieutenant Colonel Morris, commander of Det 12. The weather is FINE. Quit worrying about it and bring your plane in here. I'm getting tired of hearing Air Force excuses for why my men are still eating MREs. So get in here and land and let ME worry about the rain."

We all looked at each other in the cockpit. For a moment no one knew what to say.

"So there," said Maj Kradel.

"Sir, would it be fair to guess that Lt Col Morris is Army?" I asked.

"I think that would be fair," he answered. "Army Reserve, most likely, given his distaste for packaged food. Regular Army lives off that stuff."

"He's worrying about the weather for us," Mick added. "Guess we can stop now."

"That's a load off my mind."

"How far out?"

"Four miles."

"Roger, Snapper. You have the weather. Please make sure the runway's clear. We'll be touching down in two minutes."

"Clunk, you ready?"

"Ready. Say the word and I'll drop the ramp."

Patuca came into sight at our eleven o'clock. We were over the middle of the valley and it perched high on the left side just lower than our own altitude. We were so low we wouldn't have to descend until short final. The cloud deck sat above the field at maybe five hundred feet, gray wisps clinging to the trees on the upslope. A rain shower danced over the forest half a mile off the departure end. With it there we wouldn't have been able to land in the opposite direction even if someone had cut down the trees.

"Are the passengers clear?" I asked

"Clear. The major has them up front."

"Everyone's out of the way," Kradel added. "Make it a soft touchdown."

"Always. Mick, do you want to fly the approach?"

"Does a lobster wear a bikini?"

"Fine, I'll do it."

"You have the aircraft. And there's the runway."

"On the approach," I called and pulled the power to idle. The nose immediately tried to come down so I clicked the trim switch in the opposite direction. The airspeed fell toward one hundred.

"You're clear on the ramp, Clunk."

"Clear! Ramp's coming open!"

A *shoonk!* came from the back as the ramp locked into place.

"Ramp's open."

We could hear Clunk scrambling to the front of the cabin to get behind the pallets.

"Ready at the release!"

"Standby."

On short final the trees dropped away quickly into the river basin. I ignored them and flew right at the runway.

"You want the lift dumpers?" Mick asked, nervous as the ground got closer.

"No, we're not stopping."

"Oh, right."

"Standby," I called.

A stray sheet of verga hit the windscreen. For a moment everything outside went blurry. When the drops blew clear ground filled the picture outside. Grass at the threshold of the runway turned to gravel in the touchdown zone and then dirt after that, two worn streaks that stretched half a mile across the bluff with a slight hump between them. There were long puddles in the streaks. Grass everywhere in the camp was wet, reflecting dull light. Far down the strip someone sprinted out of the way.

"Three seconds!"

Chunk!!

The touchdown was softer than usual and I let the nose down harder than I should have. The aircraft pivoted on the main gear, pounding down on the nose gear and making it feel like we made two landings. Mick and I lurched forward in our seats. Behind us I heard more than one person get thrown against the bulkhead.

"Stand by to release!"

"Stand by!"

The driveway to the Ecuadorian camp flashed past on our left. The American tents were on the right side of the strip, more toward the center. I hesitated, wanting to slow down as much as possible and to be careful we didn't rush ourselves. If we worked it right, we would drop the pallets right in front of them.

"Get ready, Clunk! 3...2...1...Release!"

Clunk yanked on the handle. We heard the satisfying jolt of the dual rail locks retracting, then the heavy rumble of pallets sliding on rollers. The food was on its way.

But the pallets weren't sliding fast enough.

"Bastards!"

That was Clunk. Had I dared to look over my shoulder I would have seen him jump to his feet to shove on the last pallet. Mick did look back. He immediately threw off his shoulder harness and leaped out of the cockpit to help.

The problem was physics.

Although the floor of the C-27 cabin slopes aft, combat offloads normally rely on breaking inertia to get pallets moving. When the plane lurches forward, the pallets try to stay where they are. The aircraft literally drives out from underneath them.

But in our case we were already moving. And slowing down. In a frictionless world on perfect bearings, the minute Clunk unlocked the hooks our pallets would have sailed off the ramp and out of the plane. In the real world, the pallets weren't stupid. Physics let them in on the secret that they were bouncing along on an uneven strip at seventy miles per hour and that the floor's rollers, though smooth, weren't smooth enough. The pallets needed a nudge.

"Push!" I heard Clunk's desperate cry.

He pushed. So did Mick and Kradel and any admin troop who wasn't so petrified they couldn't let go of their seat belt. Alone up front I watched the end of the strip get closer. The power levers begged me to push them up.

The pallets started to move. Everyone pushed from the back, twisting their faces away from the stench of the meat. Together the three loads started to slide aft. Just after passing the American command tent the first one went out the back. I heard it go, a retreating rumble that suddenly ceased altogether. The second pallet flew out seconds after the first. Then...

The last rumble stopped. I heard yelling. Giving myself five seconds to initiate the go-around, I chanced a quick look into the cabin.

The meat pallet was stuck.

It had been sliding along fine following the path of its two colleagues when suddenly it jammed just as it passed the hinge of the ramp.

Now it was stuck two feet short of leaving the plane. Maybe the guys had shoved unevenly, maybe the pallet was warped. Whatever the reason, it jammed. That happened sometimes. It's just that now was a bad time. The end of the runway was too close for comfort and I needed to apply power.

"We have to go-around!" I called. Then, realizing everyone was off-comm, I pushed my boom mike out of the way and yelled, "Clear!"

Clunk grabbed Mick and Kradel and hauled them toward the front of the plane. With the pallet in the way, he couldn't close the ramp and could only make sure no one was at risk of falling out.

I pushed the power levers all the way forward. The engines screamed and the blades dug at the air, sending tornado-shaped contrails spinning behind the wings. We accelerated hard enough to press me against the seatback. With most of the load gone I only needed twenty knots to rotate and we got there easily.

But our center of gravity had changed. When I rotated, the nose came up faster than I expected. It was due to the weight hanging off the ramp, of course, and before I could catch it the edge of the ramp scraped the ground as we got airborne. It wasn't much of a scrape, just enough to feel it up front. Just enough to let me know I'd screwed up.

"Get the load secure!" I called into the mike.

But it was too late for that. I hauled back on the stick to clear the trees and simultaneously banked right to miss the rain shower. It was a steep enough climb-out that Mick couldn't get back into the cockpit. With one foot on the step, he was left grasping the door-rail for support.

Clunk sat on his butt and slid down the cabin floor headed for the pallet, a tie-down chain in hand. But the scrape and the jinking had an effect. He was still ten feet away when the long-suffering carcass finally made its escape. The pallet slipped free.

I felt it go. Immediately the pitch-up was easier to control. Nobody needed to tell me what that meant.

Mick stood on the cockpit step looking back in amazement. Clunk sat forlornly in the cabin, locked to his gunner's belt, the un-needed chain in his hands. The view out the open ramp framed his silhouette. In that view, the end of the airstrip slid out of sight and jungle took its place. Jungle that the pallet dove toward like a lawn dart heading for the grass. It disappeared into the trees as though swallowed.

I stayed in a 60-degree bank, turning inside the shower and bringing the C-27 around to point up the valley. We reached downwind before anyone spoke.

"Um…where did it go?"

"Down," was the response. "It went down."

Mick climbed into his seat and looked out the right window. "Into the jungle," he murmured. "I don't even see where it hit." He paused. "You think they'll still want it?"

Maj Kradel walked to the ramp and looked outside. Rain swirled around the fuselage to create a vortex behind us, making him look like he was standing inside a running hose. He stroked his moustache.

"You know," he said. "That was a big piece of beef."

3. Idiots

LOWELL HENDRICKS AND I flew up to Guatemala City one day to show the flag. We were carrying a pallet of stuff for the embassy – a copier, a paper shredder, some car parts and electrical equipment, even a case of toilet paper – but that wasn't the real reason for our trip. The real reason was that the ambassador was trying to convince the Guatemalan government to allow U.S. forces to operate in the country. Guatemala was the last link in the chain of drug transportation before the smugglers got into Mexico and there were suspected transshipment points in the country that the DEA wanted to scope out and maybe raid. Worse, the drug activity was increasing. The U.S. worried that without strong action to nip it in the bud Guatemala would suffer more and more from the traffickers and their money. The Guatemalans weren't so keen, so by bringing our small, innocuous C-27 to La Aurora International Airport we were planting the seed, showing that this was all the U.S. wanted – a chance to be around, have influence, and promote order, professionalism, and lawful behavior.

Besides, there was a Wendy's Hamburger stand that had just opened across the street from the terminal. Lowell carried a list of orders from a dozen people back in Panama.

The day was sunny and as usual the winds were strong. La Aurora sat on an Acropolis-like hill in the center of the city and caught breezes from every direction.

The airfield had other challenges. There were deep ravines on two sides of the field. There were also hills to the north. When the sun was low shadows from the hills streaked across the landscape like tiger stripes and disguised where the ravines ended and the airport began. Even when there were no shadows it was hard to make out ripples in the land due to the dense population. The buildings, the streets, and especially the shanty towns that crowded the ravines made one part of the ground look like any other.

But La Aurora held a special place in my heart because it was part of the reason I had ended up in Panama.

Two years earlier in my pilot training class I had ranked well enough to pick the aircraft of my choice on assignment night. Unfortunately, the group of planes the Air Force offered me and my classmates that month was limited: no fighters, no attack planes, no fast-movers at all.

Not even any bombers. We could choose from a list of big, fat, lumbering, heavy cargo planes and only from that list. All of us were disappointed. A few guys were flat-out crushed. One was so heartbroken we put him on suicide watch. (Years later he justified our suspicions by flying his plane into a mountain.)

But one plane on the list caught my attention: the C-27. No one knew much about it except that it was so new it was still being built, would be assigned to the South American theater, and was rumored to be a covert air job. So I chose it for my assignment.

After assignment night, one by one my fellow students received orders to their new bases. I received nothing. I waited and waited while friends packed their bags, loaded their cars, and moved away from our training base in Arizona. My instructor, Chumley, assured me that everything would turn out – I would be down south flying around the jungle before I knew it. He flew with me until graduation but then he, too, moved on to another assignment. Eventually I was the only one from my class left in the dorms.

Every day I went to the Personnel office and asked where my orders were: every day the airmen there said there was a delay.

Then one day word came down from the personnel headquarters in San Antonio that the Air

Force had changed its mind. The C-27 might not be fielded after all. Anyone planning to fly it needed to get a new assignment.

"What does that mean?" I asked the sergeant at Personnel. "I was planning to go south of the border. Will I get to choose another plane?"

"No, sir. It means San Antonio will choose one for you."

So I waited.

Waiting wasn't all bad. I got to fly – twice or three times a week the school that I had just graduated from gave me a T-38 jet to fly around for an hour or two. I passed four months that way, burning holes in the sky over the Arizona desert, doing Thunderbird rolls and pulling 6 gs while waiting for the staffers in Texas to find me a permanent job.

They tried. One day San Antonio called and offered to let me fly an F-111, a fighter-bomber that had been around since the 1960s. I jumped at the chance – it was fast, it was a combat aircraft, and it would save me from flying cargo for a living. But soon after sending me orders to report to F-111 training, a major at Personnel called to tell me they were rescinded.

"Rescinded? But why? The Air Force needs a pilot to go fly the F-111. I'm a pilot and I want to fly that plane. How can they be rescinded?"

"Sorry, lieutenant. We noticed you chose a cargo plane on your assignment night."

"So? That's all that was on the list."

"Well, that means you're a cargo pilot. Cargo pilots aren't allowed to fly fighters."

"But I'm not a cargo pilot. I've never been in a cargo plane. All I've ever flown is the jets here in school."

"Yes. That doesn't matter."

"How can it not matter? The Air Force sent me here for training. Don't they have a plan?"

"Not in Personnel, lieutenant."

"Look, I'm *not* a cargo pilot."

"On paper you are."

"What? Tear up the paper!"

But instead they tore up my orders to the F-111.

I went back to waiting. Two more months passed.

From time to time I would get calls from Personnel. Openings came up in various squadrons around the Air Force and when they did the assignment specialists in San Antonio reacted like palsy victims receiving electric shocks. First they told me they would send me to a C-130. Then two days later that changed: now it was a helicopter in Wyoming. One week they said I would be an instructor pilot at the very base I was trying to leave. The next week they needed someone to fly corporate jets out of Alabama. No one seemed to know what was going on in the assignment world and no one knew what to do with me. I stayed in Arizona, flying T-38s and wondering how my limbo would end.

Then one day I received orders to a C-5 at a base outside Sacramento. A C-5 was my worse nightmare, the heaviest of the heavies, the king of the cargo world. It was where the Air Force sent guys who needed the support of a 12-man crew to get a plane in the air. But I didn't get too upset when I saw the papers because I assumed that like all the other jobs they had found for me this one would change in a week. It didn't.

That's how I ended up in a C-5 for my first assignment. The plane was huge and flew like apartment buildings don't. It required no skill unless pushing the autopilot button could be considered a skill. Halfway through my first flight I was bored to tears. When pilots who had been flying the plane for years complimented me on my quick mastery of the plane I fought the urge to shoot them dead. A rhesus monkey could fly the C-5 – what was there to master? But I had no choice. I moved to the base in California and dragged myself to work each day, loathe to admit what I had become. Months passed.

By the time I was assigned to a trip with Colonel Willard I had long since given up trying to show any enthusiasm for the job. By then I had volunteered eight times to transfer almost anywhere else. Each time my commander turned me down. Now all I wanted to do was finish my tour and get out of the Air Force as quickly as possible so I could apply to the Navy.

Colonel Willard was the vice-commander of Travis Air Force Base. He was a former lineman on the Academy football team, a giant of a man who had to duck his head even to board the free world's largest airplane. His manner was gruff but friendly, befitting a man who wanted to be one of the boys but also a general some day. On the trip we crewed together there were two other pilots as well, an instructor named Gillian and another new co-pilot name Franks. There were four of us because our squadron was overmanned and putting several pilots on one trip was the only way to keep us all current. Our job was to fly to New Hampshire, pick up 400 National Guardsmen, and take them to Guatemala where they were to build a road. The plan was that each of us would take turns flying with the colonel. The rest of the time we could stretch out in the crew bunks and catch some sleep.

Leaving Travis, the colonel flew first with Lieutenant Franks. Over Oklahoma the plane developed a hydraulic problem and they diverted into Altus Air Force Base to get it fixed. Altus had bad weather so the colonel flew an instrument approach to get us down on the ground. But he botched it. First he turned the wrong way in the holding pattern. Then he couldn't stay on altitude and needed vectors from the controller to stay in controlled airspace. Franks, afraid to say anything at first, by the end of the approach was practically holding the colonel's hand and barking orders. After they landed the colonel lit into his copilot for interfering. "Unprofessional, inexperienced, arrogant young pup,"...etc., etc. Franks, who had been scared to death of crashing, folded like a bad poker hand and cried on the way to the hotel.

Gillian flew with the colonel after that, first to New Hampshire and then to Miami where we had to make an unplanned stop after there was confusion over our country clearance into Guatemala. In New Hampshire the colonel taxied over a fire extinguisher. In Miami he stalled the aircraft in the turn to final approach, forcing Gillian to take the controls. Then after landing he shut down three – *three* – of our four engines when sunlight tripped the optical sensors inside their cowling, causing fire lights on our emergency panel to illuminate. Granted, none of us had ever seen sunlight do that before but the man overreacted, for not only did he close the throttles, he fired the extinguisher bottles into each engine. That cost us an extra night in Miami while mechanics cleaned the turbines. Spending the night in

Miami wouldn't have been a bad deal but we had the logistics nightmare of lodging four hundred Guardsmen to keep us from enjoying the city.

So before we even left the United States Willard had proven himself a menace. Nevertheless, for some reason Gillian let me fly with him on the leg to Guatemala.

The weather was clear all the way across the Caribbean. We had only to look outside to get to our destination. Everything went fine until we got to La Aurora.

He landed long. *Wayyyy* long. The approach was steep over the hills north of the runway and Willard complicated things by being twenty knots fast the whole way. Normally, a fully-loaded C-5 can be counted on to float like a Haitian raft – get it anywhere near the runway and it'll plunk itself onto the concrete out of sheer exhaustion. But that assumes you're at the right speed. Flowing an extra twenty knots over the wings and asking it to land is like leaving a car in neutral on a hill and asking it to stay put. So when we got down to the runway we floated. And floated and floated and floated.

At the south end of the airport's 8,000-foot runway was a deep ravine with a shanty town packed along its sides. The colonel seemed unaware of it as we flew far too long, getting closer and closer to the end of the pavement. The thousand-foot marker sped past, telling us how much of the runway we had already used. Then the two-thousand-foot marker. Then the three-thousand-foot marker. There were only eight markers and we needed some of them to stop. He fought with the controls.

"Put it down, sir," I whispered.

"I have it," he snapped in reply.

We floated at ten feet, the airspeed reluctant to depart from all our momentum. We weighed seven hundred thousand pounds, after all, and getting it to slow down was like trying to rein in a freight train. The halfway point of the runway slipped beneath us.

"We need to land," I insisted.

"Lieutenant, don't...I have it!" he repeated.

But he had nothing. His meaty hands twisted the controls as the plane waffled in ground effect, that cushion of air beneath a plane's wings that pushes them away from the surface. The throttles were already in idle so there was no more power to take out. He shoved the yoke forward to bring us down then yanked it back in uncertainty, making the 350-ton aircraft dance like a diver testing the waters with his toe. We were coming to the end of the runway and the runway had no buffer. There was no overrun – the pavement just ended. After that was a sharp drop down the most populated hill this side of a Pueblo cliff dwelling. We were so close to the shanty town I saw kids in a shack look up in alarm.

"Go around!" I called.

"No, goddammit! We're fine."

But we weren't fine, not unless plunging into a fiery holocaust was fine. We went so far down the runway that I no longer trusted the engines to spool up fast enough to fly us away. So I grabbed the yoke and shoved it forward. That's the worst way in the world to land a plane but in this case it got us to the pavement the quickest. The nose gear hit simultaneous with the main, a flat landing that took seven hundred thousand pounds of people and plane and slammed it home to Mother Earth. I honked on the brakes and at the same time jerked all four engines into reverse. The engines roared. Smoke billowed from our skidding tires. We stopped two hundred feet – one C-5 length – from the ravine.

That event by itself might not have ended my career in California. Probably, but maybe not. The icing on the cake came back at home in California two days later, after our return to the air base when a number of senior-ranking officers gathered to welcome Colonel Willard. In mixed company he glossed over the Guatamala landing and implied it was my fault. Gillian, seeing me about to explode, pulled me aside.

"Relax," he counseled.

"Relax? How can you say that?"

"Because he's a colonel and there's nothing you can do about it. Look, even bad pilots can teach you something. Why get upset over it?"

I lacked Gillian's patience. We were in the Base Operations building with dozens of people standing around who made loud enough background chatter to mask my reply. But just as I spoke the conversation lulled, allowing my voice to carry through the halls.

"Because he's a ham-handed buffoon who can't fly and almost got us killed!"

Days later the C-27 reappeared on the assignment list. My commander, anxious to move me but convinced he was ending my career by sending me to such an insignificant plane, tried to talk me into going to another C-5 base instead. Disappointed in the extreme when I refused, he pulled me aside and threw an arm around my shoulders.

"I like you, Mike," he sighed, "but you're going the wrong way in your career. You're going the wrong way."

So I always had a soft spot for the airport in Guatemala City.

Lowell flew our approach from the southeast, the surprised controller in the tower reluctant to clear us for landing until he had us in sight.

He had not received our flight plan, which happened a lot, and so had a lot of questions for us about who we were, where we had come from, what time we had taken off, etc. But when he finally saw us on a wide left downwind he was still as friendly as could be. He even tried to talk to us in English. When his pauses grew too long I tried Spanish to help him out. That led to a strange exchange where I spoke bad Spanish to him while he replied in bad English. Anyone listening on the frequency probably wondered what we were doing but it got the job done.

We parked on the military side of the airport. Across the runway an American Airlines DC-10 sat on the ramp outside the civilian terminal. A long line of passengers stood on the tarmac waiting to board it. On our side there was nothing but empty concrete and a lone DC-3 parked in the grass. The DC-3 was painted white with blue detailing and 'FAG' painted in block letters on its tail.

"'FAG?'" exclaimed Lowell as we taxied in and shut down. "What the hell is that? Why would they put that on their plane?"

"'*Fuerza Aérea de Guatemala*,'" I explained. "It means 'Guatemalan Air Force.' They can't help it if it's something bad in our language."

"Don't they have a dictionary?"

"I'm sure they do."

"Well, then they should know."

"Their dictionary is in Spanish," I pointed out.

"Zero times anything is still zero."

"What does that mean?"

Lowell rolled his eyes. "It means they're idiots."

We met the station manager, the airport official who handled flights for our embassy. He was a slender man who didn't like being out in the sun. He greeted us, helped unload the cargo, and then went on his way.

We stayed only long enough to unload and to hit the Wendy's. The locals in the restaurant gazed open-mouthed as Lowell, Sergeant Brian Wilson, and I carried enough hamburgers to feed a football team out the door.

"They think we're getting this all for ourselves," our loadmaster cackled as we crossed back over the street.

"Idiots," muttered Lowell.

There was a small kiosk on the ramp where a FAG captain we met insisted he could help us file a flight plan. He gave us a mimeographed form with print so faint I could barely read it. I filled it out as carefully as if it were the Magna Carta, then made a point of thanking the captain for going out of his way to help us. After all, the point of the trip was to make friends. He seemed pleased.

"That's their operations office?" Lowell was incredulous. "You're kidding me."

"Maybe that's all they need. How much traffic does it look like they get?"

"Yeah, but that? The guy didn't even have a phone. He didn't have a pen, either – he borrowed yours!"

"You've never borrowed a pen?"

"Oh, you're saying he *had* a pen but just misplaced it?"

"Maybe."

"Well, zero times anything is still zero."

"You said that before. What does it mean?"

"It means their base operations is a bunch of idiots."

"Hey, Mr. Negative. Is everyone an idiot?"

"It looks like it around here."

The captain waved good-bye and marshaled us out, the bright sun stretching his shadow across the pavement as he gestured with his arms.

There was one taxiway. It was on the civilian side of the field so the tower controller told us to hold our position for landing traffic. A Cessna 172 made a long slow approach from the north, landed almost directly in front of us on the runway, then taxied to a ramp down from the terminal.

"Shark 12, uhh...now you can cross the runway to the civilian side. Follow American jet to runway 18."

"Shark 12, roger."

We taxied across the runway and turned right on the parallel taxiway that ran by the civilian terminal. The American DC-10 was on its way out ahead of us. It was a huge plane and we made plenty of room for it. The blast from just one of its three engines could flip us over if we got too close so we dawdled along two to three football fields behind it. We weren't in any hurry but it was just our luck to try to depart at the same time as the only other plane at the airport. Now that the Cessna was down there wasn't even another aircraft anywhere over the city.

It was while we were taxiing out that the engine fire lights illuminated, as did the Master Fire Warning light on the panel in front of both pilots. It was like having a Christmas tree suddenly appear in the cockpit.

"Holy cats!" said Lowell, and instinctively reached for the T-handle nearest to him. The T-handles activated a valve on the fuel line going into each engine. Pulling one would shut its respective engine down in a matter of seconds.

"Whoa!" I said.

"Whoa, what? It's a fire!"

"No, wait."

Just as in the C-5, the fire warning circuit activated from optical sensors around the combustion chamber. The sensors detected light, not heat. If there were a fire outside the combustion chamber presumably it came from a fire that burned through the wall. But according to our engine temperature gauges, everything inside the chamber was fine.

"Hey, man, we'd better stop."

"Hold on a second," I said, raising a hand. "All the other instruments are normal."

"Yeah, but..."

"Wait."

The throttles were in idle and I kept my feet off the brakes. We continued to roll down the taxiway. Eventually we entered a shadow from one of the hangars. As soon as we did the fire lights went out.

Lowell and Sgt Wilson exchanged looks of surprise. We taxied back into sunshine. After several seconds the lights came on again. When we entered another shadow they went out. Brian caught on first.

"It's the sun?" he said.

"Yeah."

"How'd you know that?" Lowell demanded.

I demurred, feeling Gillian's wisdom finally sink in.

"I didn't."

"Then why didn't you let me pull the fire handles?!"

"Because we weren't on fire. Come on, what are the chances we would get fires in both engines at the same time? Zero. We must be at just the right angle to let light get in through some cowling. Besides, the other gauges look fine. As the tyrants in pilot training used to say, 'Always check the other gauges.'"

Brian made a bowing motion from the third seat.

"Ohh, god-like one. For that you deserve a chocolate frostie. You'd better hurry and get to altitude, though, if you want to eat it before it melts."

The tower cleared the DC-10 to take off. Then the controller changed his mind and cleared the airplane on to hold only, which meant the pilots could taxi onto the runway but had to wait for clearance to go any further. When the airliner started to move the controller again cleared it for take-off, then again changed his mind. The massive jet made the turn at the hammerhead and pulled onto the runway, then sat there with its engines at idle, waiting. As soon as those engines were no longer pointing their exhaust at us, we moved up to the end of the taxiway and turned ninety degrees to face the runway.

"*American 252, standby for take-off clearance,*" the controller said.

"*American 252, standing by,*" the amused voice of the American pilot came back. He had clearly been to Guatemala before.

"Oh, man, would you look at that." Brian pointed to the overrun behind the DC-10.

The overrun is an asphalt extension of the runway that leaves a big open space where aircraft taking off can run up their engines. Here at the north end of the runway the space was big enough but high bushes and trees surrounded it on three sides. What our loadmaster was pointing at was a column of men, Guatemalan army conscripts, that emerged from a dirt path among the bushes. They crossed the overrun from left to right less than a hundred feet behind the tail of the idling DC-10. There must have been fifty, crossing in single file, heading for another path on the far side. Incredibly, each carried a 4' x 8' piece of plywood, thirty-two square feet of wooden board just waiting to catch sail on the wind.

Or a blast of air.

"American 252, you are cleared for take-off," came the controller's voice, oblivious to the soldiers on the overrun.

"American 252, cleared for take-off," the pilot repeated.

"Oh, my god," Brian said, gazing open-mouthed out the window.

Lowell just shook his head. "Idiots," he muttered.

I keyed the mike.

"American 252, don't run up your engines. Don't run up your engines. You've got people behind you."

The tower controller was the first to answer.

"Who is transmitting on my frequency?"

The American jet's engines started to come up. We heard their whine above the sound of our own propellers. Just as quickly they were cut back to idle. The dozen conscripts behind the engines at that moment felt even that small blast as the exhaust caught their boards and sent them tripping and dancing across the overrun.

"*Say again?*" came the American pilot's voice.

"Who is on my frequency? American 252, you are cleared for take-off."

"Yeah, American, this is the C-27 right next to you. You've got about fifty guys walking across the overrun behind your plane. If you push up your engines you'll blow them into next week. We'll tell you when you're clear."

"Okay. Thanks for the heads-up. Tower, this is American 252. We have people on the overrun so we're going to hold our position for a moment."

"*Hmm?*" There was a long pause while the controller moved around in his greenhouse to try to see what was happening. "Okay, American 252, tell me...tell me when you are ready."

The conscripts got the clue and raced across the overrun as quickly as their burdens would allow. Apparently it never occurred to them just to stop and get clear. After several minutes the last one disappeared down the trail on the far side.

"Finally," said Lowell.

But just as I was about to key the mike two more soldiers appeared. *Sans* boards, they trotted leisurely across the asphalt after the rest of their company, blissfully oblivious to the monster airplane parked only yards away. Lowell sighed and threw up his hands, thoroughly exasperated.

"*Okay, American,*" I tried hard not to laugh into the radio. "*You're all clear.*"

"*Hey, thanks again. You guys have a great day.*"

"*We already have. You, too.*"

"*Tower, American 252 is ready for take-off now.*"

"*Roger, American 252. You are cleared for take-off. The people are all gone now?*"

"*Yes, sir. The people are all gone.*"

Lowell was beside himself.

"Idiots."

4. Weather

HOROSCOPES WITH NUMBERS. THAT'S what Walt called weather forecasts.

Walt wasn't with us, unfortunately. He was asleep in his bed back in Panama City while Evan and I droned through the night off the coast of Costa Rica in a twin-engine cargo plane, dodging some of the most fearsome thunderstorms this side of Valhalla. Our weather flimsy promised us fair skies and stars overhead but one look at the lightning outside proved that a lie. The weatherman who had given us the report earlier in the day was a cheerful airman who had probably never seen lightning in his life except from the comfort of his bedroom window. Maybe at the ripe age of nineteen he thought the occasional storm still qualified as "fair." It didn't. If Walt had been with us, he would have taken one look out the cockpit window and pronounced his verdict. Horoscopes with numbers.

"You want to turn?" Evan asked.

It was so dark that we couldn't see outside unless lightning lit up the sky, so Evan was staring at the radar. Its screen was black, too, except for a green blip that marched down its center toward us.

"What is it?" I asked.

"I don't know."

"Is it rain?"

"I don't know."

I looked outside again. The storm was off to our left. The ocean was below and to our right. We were fifty miles off the coast already and I didn't want to fly any further over the water if I could help it. I didn't like flying over the water, especially at night.

"Maybe it's nothing," Evan suggested. He was even newer than me and he had narcolepsy to boot. Since he slept through most of his flights, the fact that he was even looking at the radar tonight was a novel experience.

"Yeah, maybe."

The weather is a beautiful irony in the tropics. The same environmental factors that produce dazzling sunny days also create storms of volcanic fury. Solar heating, the earth's rotation, upper-level winds, mountains, oceans, and the occasional El Niño work the latitudes from Ecuador to Guatemala the way Mongol hordes used to work rural villages.

The storms they create are different from those in the States. In northern climes thunderstorms usually appear as part of a front, a line of unstable air that sucks in moisture to rise with its heat, creating bumpy cauliflower shapes that grow dark with rain and rumble echoes of thunder from Ohio to Missouri. Sometimes that happened in Central America but more often the hazard was a single cumulus buildup, the 'white puffie' that got carried away and swelled to twice the size of Everest. These floated ominously around the sky hiding the violence within their mass, looking for a pressure system or a mountain to smack into so they could dump their rain and give vent to the thunder and lightning and rushing winds inside.

During the day we learned to watch for clues that there might be storms inside a random cloud. Gray was the warning that rain – and therefore powerful downdrafts – was inside. Updrafts went with any cumulus cloud. They were what made the cloud and gave it its haphazard, blooming shape. But when the updrafts met the downdrafts, that's when things got ugly. Together these roaring columns of air could rip an aircraft apart. It was like being hit by elevators going in opposite directions.

During the day that gray color was often the only sign that one cloud was not like the others, that somewhere along the line it had fallen into evil ways and now was beckoning with one hand while hiding a knife in the other. That recognition was important because we flew in the middle altitudes of 10,000 to 25,000 feet where thunderstorm activity is common and lightning even more so. Instead of flying over storms we usually had to dodge between them like a pedestrian sidestepping a fight.

At night storms were harder to dodge because we couldn't see them. That's why Evan was glued to the radar.

"Step out the range," I suggested.

Evan adjusted the radar to see eighty miles in front of us. The green blip disappeared, then – as the pie-like sweep returned – reappeared in the middle of the scope. It was just a tiny rectangular blip, the kind that would appear if we were low over the ocean and the radar waves reflected off a boat. Since we were now at 17,000 feet, it probably wasn't a boat.

I scowled at the radar, thinking. It had been a long day. We had started out at 6 a.m. in Honduras doing parachute training with Honduran soldiers, half of whom ignored the loadmaster's instructions and jumped before he wanted them to. They landed in trees, in water, in a swamp, everywhere but where they should have, and it took us hours to land and collect them all.

Then we had picked up a load of Rangers and brought them back to Panama, a three-hour flight that we thought would end the day. But the Air Operations Center had sent us back to Honduras to pick up a second load of troops.

Now we were on our way home for the second time.

The flights were cake, exactly the kind I hated: long, boring drones just to carry ground-pounders from one place to another. The only thing that kept us on our toes was the weather. To get to Honduras and back we had to pass Costa Rica and for some reason that little country seemed to grow thunderstorms the way Alaskan summers grow mosquitos. Huge thunderstorms formed over San Jose early in the evening. By the time we headed back to Panama they were monsters, 60,000 feet tall and shooting lightning in all directions. We found that by deviating over the water we could stay clear but as the storms grew so did our deviations. By ten o'clock at night we had been flying for sixteen hours. Everyone was tired and wanted the shortest route home.

"You want to turn?" Evan repeated.

"No, not yet."

He frowned and settled back in his seat. Evan had a reputation for being able to sleep under the most stressful of circumstances – he had dozed off once during a check ride – but now even he couldn't relax. The green blip loomed in his vision.

Most guys I flew with took weather so seriously that we never even used the phrase *bad weather*. There was no such thing as *bad weather*. There was just *weather*. If the sky outside was sunny and dry and you could see forever then it wasn't *weather*. It was a nice day. If on the other hand it was overcast, raining, and supposed to stay that way for a while, only then was it *weather*. And if thunderstorms crowded the sky like drunks packing a bar and lightning flashed all over and hail pounded the aircraft so hard you thought it would crash through the windscreen, then it was *real weather*, as in "We ran into some real weather coming back from Bogotá last night – the loadmaster pissed his pants and we thought we were going to die."

There was no predicting weather in the region, good or bad, except to say that it could always be out there. Even the weather squadron on the air base gave up trying. The weather squadron was in the base operations building a hundred yards from our hangar, where pilots filed flight plans and received pre-flight briefings on what they could expect from the skies along their route. Except our meteorologists were so lacking in the most basic observational tools of the trade that they usually avoided talking to pilots for fear of having their knowledge vacuum exposed. Senior forecasters would see us approach the briefing desk and scatter in guilty haste, leaving only the lowest-ranking airman to hand us a weather flimsy and translate its message.

"Isolated thunderstorms enroute, sir," the airman would always say, flashing a helpless smile as he traced his fingers enthusiastically across pages packed with numbers and squiggly lines that he may or may not have understood.

Sometimes whoever it was would forego any pretense at prognostication and save time by just calling out the cover-your-ass phrase as we came through the door. "Isolated thunderstorms enroute!" We started using it as a greeting, pronouncing the words in unison with the airman as we approached the desk.

On occasion the forecaster would actually wait to learn our destination. He would then take several minutes to pore over pressure-gradient charts and winds aloft reports and to stare at radar screens before announcing the same thing. Only once did I hear anything different. One day before a flight to Colombia with Little Bud a forecaster told us there would be "isolated thunderstorms *most* of the way." Little Bud eyed the kid warily and inquired what we would see on the rest of the trip. "Oh, sir," the earnest blue-suiter replied, "*scattered* thunderstorms everywhere else."

Horoscopes with numbers.

The C-27 radar worked like any other. It showed images on the screen if the waves it sent out hit something and bounced back. The images varied in color based on how solid the object was. Green appeared if the waves encountered light rain, meaning most of the waves penetrated the shower and only a few came back. Yellow appeared if the rain was heavy, meaning water reflected most of the radar signal. Red came up if none of the radar waves was able to penetrate and all came bouncing back. In that case the rain was nothing you wanted to mess with. Such cells usually appeared as a red dot or splotch surrounded by yellow, a meteorological bloodshot eye to be avoided at all cost.

So green usually wasn't that bad.

"There's nothing around it," Evan said cautiously, stifling a yawn.

A psychologist would have called Evan's statement a 'trial balloon,' the kind of thing one says when, not being sure, one wants to elicit a thoughtful, helpful response from someone else before acting.

I didn't say anything helpful. I said, "Hmm."

The Air Force also has a basic flying regulation for all its pilots, one that includes a sentence that says, "There is no reason to fly through a thunderstorm in peacetime."

We kept flying directly at the blip. It was uncanny. Even when Evan stepped the radar to its maximum range of 160 miles the blip was the only thing that showed up – and it was right in our flight path. It was now 30 miles away.

I looked at the map. Howard Air Base, our destination, was 62 miles away, ten minutes in a straight line on the other side of the blip. If we flew around the blip we would no longer be flying a straight line.

"What do you think?" he said.

I knew what I thought. I wanted to get home.

A bolt of lightning from the storm off to our left shot across the sky above us. For a brief second it lit up the world but came so fast and so bright that it blinded us rather than helped us see anything out front. The storm over there was growing.

"I don't really want to deviate," I said.

Evan waffled, too. "I definitely don't want to go any further out over the water," he agreed.

"Me, neither."

Jamie Tunkelmann, our loadmaster, stuck his head through the curtain that blocked off the cargo compartment.

"Hey, sir, how much longer? This day feels like it's never going to end."

"About fifteen minutes," I told him, then pointed at the radar screen. "What do you make of that?"

He squinted at the screen. "What is it, Pac-Man?"

"I hope not."

"Is it rain?"

"Either that or the Goodyear Blimp is lost."

He shrugged it off. "If it's rain, who cares?"

"We were just trying to decide if it's a storm or not."

"Storms are red, aren't they?"

"Yeah, usually."

"Well, hey, I don't care. You guys are the pilots. Do that magic thing you do and just get me on the ground. These Army guys are driving me nuts."

"They're not sleeping?"

"Nah, they're all over the place – the floor, the seats, the pallets. I don't care about that but they spilled the cooler and somehow they managed to plug up the pisser so now nobody can use it. How do you plug up a pisser? We've only got so many Gatorade bottles lying around, for god's sake. And some idiot back here keeps telling me I tied their bags down wrong."

"What do you know?" Evan taunted. "You throw little Honduran guys into trees."

"Yeah, I'm a bastard, aren't I? Let's land, please. Make the bad man stop. I need a drink."

The blip was now at twenty miles. At 220 knots airspeed we were moving along about four miles a minute. My brain lapse continued.

"It's just a rain shower," I decided. "We'll go through it."

"Yeah," said Evan. "It'll go right by. In and out in thirty seconds."

The blip marched closer. Evan stepped the range to 20 miles, then to 10, pushing the blip back up the screen but causing it to grow larger each time and giving it greater detail. Now it curved inward with stubby bull's horns pointing in our direction.

"Is there a shadow back there?" I asked suddenly. I leaned forward and punched the range button back to 20 miles.

Sometimes with very heavy showers the radar waves scatter off the first drops they hit and never have a chance to penetrate to tell you what's beyond the front face of a storm. Usually that happens with yellow splotches, rain that's obviously heavy to begin with, but it can happen with green ones. The tell-tale sign is a line of showers that shows up as a thin green line followed by a broader yellow one followed by some spots of red. Except that in some places the yellow and the red don't follow the green. Instead there's a suspicious part of the front line behind which is only blackness, suggesting that the ranks have been weakened there and that if you break through at that spot you'll be home free. It's like an enemy army trying to tempt you onto the field by showing just a few soldiers when behind the next hill lurks their whole Home Guard.

"No," said Evan, uncertainty back in his voice. Two minutes to go.

"Hey, Jamie?"

"Sir?"

"Tell those guys to strap in."

"Weather?"

"I don't know, but just to be safe... And tell them to be quick about it."

Evan looked at me. I looked back and shrugged. It was just a green area, I insisted to myself. We flew through those all the time. All that happened was that we got wet.

"We can still turn," Evan suggested. We couldn't, actually, because the horns now reached out either side of us.

"Nah," I tried to sound nonchalant. "It's narrow right there at the 11 o'clock. We'll go through there."

The front line of the blip merged with the bottom of the radar scope. On the 10-mile scope the blip disappeared as though we had eaten it. In 2.5-mile, though, the scope filled with green. Rain pattered against the windscreen.

"Pilot, Load, the pax are secure."

"Thanks, Jamie."

The rain fell harder.

"Well," said Evan carefully, "twenty seconds inside it and so far noth—"

His words were sucked out of his throat as the plane suddenly dropped fifty feet. At the bottom it was brought up short as though jerked on a string.

Thrown about in my seat I pulled back on the controls, which had no effect whatsoever. Before anyone could say anything we were thrown back upward. The plane lurched into a thirty-degree left bank but we kept climbing. The altimeter went crazy. We shot straight up through 18,000 feet and kept going. The vertical velocity indicator, which measured our climb rate, bounced around like a compass in an iron mine.

"Holy s...!" someone yelled.

Our altitude jumped to 19,600 feet before leveling off. Immediately we started back down.

"We're slowing down," Evan managed to say.

"I know...'"

I cranked hard right on the yoke to bring us back to level flight. The controls answered but I overshot. Now we dropped through 16,000 feet in a hellacious downdraft in twenty degrees right bank.

"Goddammit," I muttered, and corrected. Evan pushed up the props and the C-27 roared its power above the sound of the rain. The VVI finally found some self-control and pegged itself at the bottom of the gauge, over six thousand feet per minute descent. We were dropping like a potted plant but there was nothing to do except be grateful we were over the ocean and had three miles below us to spare. The goal was to fly out of the downdraft before we ran out of altitude.

"Fifteen thousand," Evan called, holding tightly to his seat with both hands. His approach book came out of its holder and hit him in the face.

The airspeed needle jumped back and forth. The turbulence got so bad it was hard to tell which way we were pointing. We struggled to read the artificial horizon and keep our wings level. That's what the regulation said to do in situations like this – the same regulation that said not to fly through thunderstorms. The rule's exact verbiage eluded me but an instructor had once phrased it like this: "If you're bouncing around, hold the plane level. Nobody has ever collided with the air."

The rain increased. It poured off the windscreen in waves.

"Fourteen thousand...thirteen-five...thirteen thousand..."

The VVI came off the bottom peg. It wavered near minus 4. We felt our fall decelerate. When the needle came back to zero and hesitated, I took advantage of the calm to adjust the throttles higher.

The needle bounced to +1.

"Going up," I said into the mike.

There was a nudge from the back as though the plane was pushed up from the tail to balance on its nose. The artificial horizon actually showed our nose moving into the black – which meant we were pointing down – but the VVI showed the opposite. With that nod toward the ocean below, the whole plane abruptly shot upward. An invisible giant hand pushed us down into the seats.

"Oh, man!" Evan groaned. He tried to lean forward to change the range on the radar but g-forces held him back. Not that the radar would have helped any. We were catching so much rain the screen had strobed. It sent broken lines in all directions, the electronic equivalent of throwing up its hands.

"Don't...worry, guys, we should...be almost... out of it," I managed to say.

And then we were.

The aircraft leveled off. The radar worked normally again, the sweep of the transmitter clearing away the pixilation like nuisance leaves from a patio. The green blotch was gone and the rain on the windscreen blew away. The scope showed an empty sky before us. Suddenly, all was quiet.

I checked the engine gauges. Everything was within limits.

Evan adjusted his headphones and stared into the blackness. "Whooah," he exhaled.

I kept my hands on the controls. My grip was so tight that if the yoke had been alive I would have choked it.

We ended up at just over 18,000 feet. Thirty miles away the lights of Panama City twinkled just as they did on any beautiful tropical night.

"Is that over?" came Jamie's voice over the intercom.

I sure as hell hoped so. "Yes. Is everyone alright back there?" I had a nightmare vision of bodies sprawled around the cabin.

"Oh, yeah. Goddamned Army guys. They're laughing like it's a carnival ride. A real roller coaster. One guy took his seatbelt off so he could fly around the cabin. They're patching him up now. Another one pissed all over because he tried to fill a Gatorade bottle when I told him to wait. I hate these guys." He poked his head through the curtain. "Hey, nothing personal but if that's the magic thing you guys do then don't do it anymore, okay? If there are any more storms out there that can pick up our 50,000 pounds of movin'-stupid and bitch-slap it across the sky, let's fly around them. I don't need that kind of excitement."

"Right. Sorry about that."

He shook his head and dropped back into the cabin. Jamie had flown with new pilots before.

For a while Evan and I were quiet. I began a shallow descent toward the coast.

"You want to fly the approach?" I offered. I needed to unlock my grip from the controls.

"No, no. You've got it."

"Okay, but take the controls for a minute so I can stretch."

"Yeah, okay. Co-pilot's controls."

"Co-pilot's controls."

Whew. I rubbed my hands on my legs to loosen them up. My heart rate continued down from triple digits. The knowledge that I had just put us into a dangerous situation was bad enough but the real stress came from being in a plane that was out of control. Whenever a plane leaped and yanked and jerked and sped up and slowed down I wanted it to be because I was making it do those things, not because Mother Nature was bouncing me like a puppet on a string. A roller coaster, hell. I would take a roller coaster any day.

"My controls again."

"Your controls."

I settled in and determined to fly a perfect landing back at Howard.

"Hey."

"Hmm?" said Evan.

I looked out the window. Except for the city lights the world was black. The lightning was behind us now, only occasionally reflecting desperate flashes off the metal of my window frame. With jungle now to the left and ocean to the right, the horizons could have been outer space.

"The next time we see a blip like that and you ask me if I want to go around it..."

"Mm-hmm?"

"Make sure I say yes."

There was a long moment where he didn't answer. When I looked over he was asleep.

ABOUT THE AUTHOR

Michael Bleriot is a military and civilian pilot. For several years he flew tactical airlift in Central and South America, supporting local militaries and U.S. forces in their attempts to limit the production and distribution of illegal drugs.

www.ingramcontent.com/pod-product-compliance
Lightning Source LLC
LaVergne TN
LVHW041613070426
835507LV00008B/214